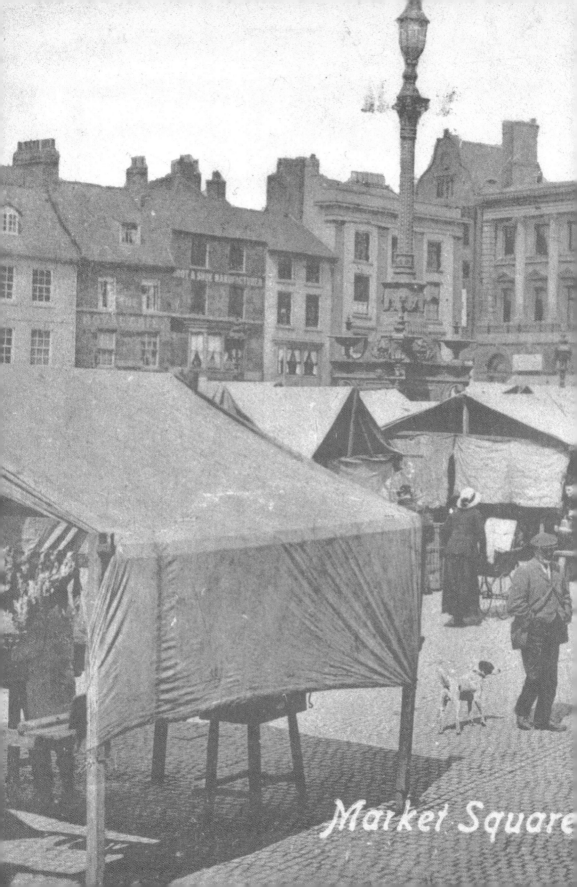

Market Square

m East. Northampton

A CENTURY *of*
NORTHAMPTON

The old fountain in the Market Square in the spring of 1962, shortly before it was declared unsafe and demolished. It was put up in 1863 to mark the marriage of the Prince of Wales to Princess Alexandra of Denmark and was presented to the town by Captain Isaacs, Commanding Officer of the 5th Corps Northampton Volunteers.

A CENTURY *of*
NORTHAMPTON

ROBERT COOK

SUTTON PUBLISHING

This book was first published in 1999 by Sutton Publishing Limited.

This new paperback edition first published in 2007 by
Sutton Publishing, an imprint of NPI Media Group
Cirencester Road · Chalford · Stroud · Gloucestershire · GL6 8PE

British Library Cataloguing in Publication Data
A catalogue record for this book is available from the British Library.

ISBN 978-0-7509-4929-3

Front endpaper: A view from the east of the Market Square in Edwardian times, with the Emporium Arcade recently completed. It seems as if the main business of the day is at its end, with time to stop and chat before enjoying a leisurely stroll home.

Back endpaper: Northampton Market Place seen from the Grosvenor Centre car park. There is talk of demolishing Greyfriars bus station and Mayorhold car park to double the size of the Grosvenor, with buses boosted by a rapid transit system. Whatever the pace of life in Northampton in the past, change still seems to be the watchword for the foreseeable future.

Half title page: The cross built by Edward I near Delapre Abbey to mark one of his five stopping places en route from Harby, near Lincoln, to Westminster with the body of his beloved wife Eleanor of Castile in 1290. He ordered what are now known as Eleanor Crosses to be built along the way, and this one was designed by John de la Bataille. It stands on the edge of the former abbey grounds, which are now Delapre Park. The abbey was built by the second Earl of Northampton, Simon de Senlis, in 1145, and in the thirteenth and fourteenth centuries it housed nuns of the Cluniac order, a reformed branch of the Benedictines. Two other Eleanor Crosses survive, at Geddington and Waltham.

Title page: Charles Bradlaugh's statue looks down on Abington Square. Bradlaugh first stood for parliament in 1868, but did not reach Westminster until Gladstone's Liberals' victory of 1880. He refused to take the oath of allegiance on the Bible, and it was not before he was prosecuted, imprisoned and expelled from the House that he established the right of atheists to affirm. The strongly Christian Gladstone found him a thorn in the side, but Northampton went on to re-elect him four times. He aroused such passions that when the Conservatives won a by-election in October 1874, largely because of a split Liberal vote, Bradlaugh's supporters attacked the followers of the moderate Liberal candidate Fowler and damaged the offices of the newspaper that backed him. The disturbances were one of the first major tests of a town police force formed in 1849.

Typeset in Photina.
Typesetting and origination by
Sutton Publishing.
Printed and bound in England.

Contents

Queen Elizabeth tours Church's shoe factory in St James after taking lunch at the Guildhall on 8 July 1965. Managing director Stewart Kennedy is leading the tour and the Queen is followed by the Lord Lieutenant of Northamptonshire, the seventh Earl Spencer, grandfather of the present Earl and the late Princess Diana. The Queen's next visit was to Althorp, the Earl's family home since 1508 and a house with which Prince Charles would become familiar when courting first Sarah Spencer and later Diana. Church and Co. still makes shoes for a very discerning clientele, but the family no longer has a majority holding in the company and in the autumn of 1999 there was speculation that French and Italian companies were interested in buying the firm.

Britain: A Century
of Change

Children gathered around an early wireless set in the 1920s. The speed and forms of communication were to change dramatically as the century advanced. (*Barnaby's Picture Library*)

The delirious rejoicing at the news of the Relief of Mafeking, during the Boer War in May 1900, is a colourful historical moment. But, in retrospect, the introduction that year of the first motor bus was rather more important, signalling another major adjustment to town life. In the previous 60 years railway stations, post-and-telegraph offices, police and fire stations, gas works and gasometers, new livestock markets and covered markets, schools, churches, football grounds, hospitals and asylums, water pumping stations and sewerage plants had totally altered the urban scene, as the country's population tripled and over 70 per cent were born in or moved to the towns.

When Queen Victoria died in 1901, she was measured for her coffin by her grandson Kaiser Wilhelm, the London prostitutes put on black mourning and the blinds came down in the villas and terraces spreading out from the old town centres. These centres were reachable by train and tram, by the new bicycles and still newer motor cars, connected by the new telephone, and lit by gas or even electricity. The shops may have been full of British-made cotton and woollen clothing but the grocers and butchers were selling cheap Danish bacon, Argentinian beef, Australasian mutton, tinned or dried fish and fruit from Canada, California and South Africa. Most of these goods were carried in British-built-and-crewed ships, burning Welsh steam coal.

As the first decade moved on, the Open Spaces Act meant more parks, bowling greens and cricket pitches. The first state pensions came in, together with higher taxation and death duties. These were raised mostly to pay for the new Dreadnought battleships needed to maintain naval superiority over Germany, and deter them from war. But the deterrent did not work. The First World War transformed the place of women, as they took over many men's jobs. Its other legacies were the war memorials which joined the statues of Victorian worthies in main squares round the land. After 1918 death duties bit even harder and a quarter of England changed hands in a few years.

Women working as porters on the Great Western Railway, Paddington, *c.* 1917. (*W.L. Kenning/ Adrian Vaughan Collection*)

The multiple shop – the chain store – appeared in the high street: Sainsburys, Maypole, Lipton's, Home & Colonial, the Fifty Shilling Tailor, Burton, Boots, W.H. Smith. The shopper was spoilt for choice, attracted by the brash fascias and advertising hoardings for national brands like Bovril, Pears Soap, and Ovaltine. Many new buildings began to be seen, such as garages, motor showrooms, picture palaces (cinemas), 'palais de dance', and the bow-windowed, pebble-dashed, tile-hung, half-timbered houses that were built as ribbon-development along the roads and new bypasses or on the new estates nudging the green belts.

During the 1920s cars became more reliable and sophisticated as well as commonplace, with developments like the electric self-starter making them easier for women to drive. Who wanted to turn a crank handle in the new short skirt? This was, indeed, the electric age as much as the motor era. Trolley buses, electric trams and trains extended mass transport and electric light replaced gas in the street and the home, which itself was groomed by the vacuum cleaner.

A major jolt to the march onward and upward was administered by the Great Depression of the early 1930s. The older British industries – textiles, shipbuilding, iron, steel, coal – were already under pressure from foreign competition when this worldwide slump arrived, cutting exports by half in two years and producing 3 million unemployed (and still rising) by 1932. Luckily there were new diversions to alleviate the misery. The 'talkies' arrived in the cinemas; more and more radios and gramophones were to be found in people's homes; there were new women's magazines, with fashion, cookery tips and problem pages; football pools; the flying feats of women pilots like Amy Johnson; the Loch Ness Monster; cheap chocolate and the drama of Edward VIII's abdication.

Father and child cycling past Buckingham Palace on VE Day, 8 May 1945. (*Hulton Getty Picture Collection*)

Things were looking up again by 1936 and unemployment was down to 2 million. New light industry was booming in the Home Counties as factories struggled to keep up with the demand for radios, radiograms, cars and electronic goods including the first television sets. The threat from Hitler's Germany meant rearmament, particularly of the airforce, which stimulated aircraft and aero engine firms. If you were lucky and lived in the south, there was good money to be earned. A semi-detached house cost £450, a Morris Cowley £150. People may have smoked like chimneys but life expectancy, since 1918, was up by 15 years while the birth rate had almost halved. The fifty-four hour week was down to forty-eight hours and there were 9 million radio licences by 1939.

In some ways it is the little memories that seem to linger longest from the Second World War: the kerbs painted white to show up in the blackout, the rattle of ack-ack shrapnel on roof tiles, sparrows killed by bomb blast, painting your legs brown and then adding a black seam down the back to simulate stockings. The biggest damage, apart from

A family gathered around their television set in the 1950s. (*Hulton Getty Picture Collection*)

London, was in the south-west (Plymouth, Bristol) and the Midlands (Coventry, Birmingham). Postwar reconstruction was rooted in the Beveridge Report which set out the expectations for the Welfare State. This, together with the nationalisation of the Bank of England, coal, gas, electricity and the railways, formed the programme of the Labour government in 1945. At this time the USA was calling in its debts and Britain was beggared by the war, yet still administering its Empire.

Times were hard in the late 1940s, with rationing even more stringent than during the war. Yet this was, as has been said, 'an innocent and well-behaved era'. The first let-up came in 1951 with the Festival of Britain and then there was another fillip in 1953 from the Coronation, which incidentally gave a huge boost to the spread of TV. By 1954 leisure motoring had been resumed but the Comet – Britain's best hope for taking on the American aviation industry – suffered a series of mysterious crashes. The Suez debacle of 1956 was followed by an acceleration in the withdrawal from Empire, which had begun in 1947 with the Independence of India. Consumerism was truly born with the advent of commercial TV and most homes soon boasted washing machines, fridges, electric irons and fires.

The *Lady Chatterley* obscenity trial in 1960 was something of a straw in the wind for what was to follow in that decade. A collective loss of inhibition seemed to sweep the land, as stately home owners opened up, the Beatles and the Rolling Stones transformed popular music, and retailing, cinema and the theatre were revolutionised. Designers, hairdressers, photographers and models moved into places vacated by an Establishment put to flight by the new breed of satirists spawned by *Beyond the Fringe* and *Private Eye*.

In the 1970s Britain seems to have suffered a prolonged hangover after the excesses of the previous decade. Ulster, inflation and union troubles were not made up for by entry into the EEC, North Sea Oil, Women's Lib or, indeed, Punk Rock. Mrs Thatcher applied the corrective in the 1980s, as the country moved more and more from its old manufacturing base over to providing services, consulting, advertising, and expertise in the 'invisible' market of high finance or in IT. Britain entertained the world with *Cats*, *Phantom of the Opera*, *Four Weddings and a Funeral*, *The Full Monty*, *Mr Bean* and the *Teletubbies*.

The post-1945 townscape has seen changes to match those in the worlds of work, entertainment and politics. In 1956 the Clean Air Act served notice on smogs and pea-souper fogs, smuts and blackened buildings, forcing people to stop burning coal and go over to smokeless sources of heat and energy. In the same decade some of the best urban building took place in the 'new towns' like Basildon, Crawley, Stevenage and Harlow. Elsewhere open warfare was declared on slums and what was labelled inadequate, cramped, back-to-back, two-up, two-down, housing. The new 'machine for living in' was a flat in a high-rise block. The architects and planners who promoted these were in league with the traffic engineers, determined to keep the motor car moving whatever the price in multi-storey car parks, meters, traffic wardens and ring roads.

Carnaby Street in the 1960s. (*Barnaby's Picture Library*)

The Millennium Dome at Greenwich, 1999. (*Michael Durnan/Barnaby's Picture Library*)

The old pollutant, coal smoke, was replaced by petrol and diesel exhaust, and traffic noise. Even in the back garden it was hard to find peace as motor mowers, then leaf blowers and strimmers made themselves heard, and the neighbours let you share their choice of music from their powerful new amplifiers, whether you wanted to or not. Fast food was no longer only a pork pie in a pub or fish-and-chips. There were Indian curry houses, Chinese take-aways and American-style hamburgers, while the drinker could get away from beer in a wine bar. Under the impact of television the big Gaumonts and Odeons closed or were rebuilt as multi-screen cinemas, while the palais de dance gave way to discos and clubs.

From the late 1960s the introduction of listed buildings and conservation areas, together with the growth of preservation societies, put a brake on 'comprehensive redevelopment'. Now the new risk at the end of the 1990s is that town centres may die, as shoppers are attracted to the edge-of-town supermarkets surrounded by parking space, where much more than food and groceries can be bought. The ease of the one-stop shop represents the latest challenge to the good health of our towns. But with care, ingenuity and a determination to keep control of our environment, this challenge can be met.

Northampton: An Introduction

To the visitor, Northampton first appears as modern suburbs; but is has ancient roots, as the New Towns Commission and its Development Corporation discovered in the 1960s, when they cleared the way for a mass influx of newcomers from London and elsewhere. They uncovered much of antiquity, and unhappily removed much of it, too.

The town's origins have been traced back to Belinus, a British king. Traces of early occupation have been found in Danes Camp on Hunsbury Hill, south-west of town. Northamptonshire was part of the Saxon kingdom of Mercia, which in AD 870 was overrun by the Danes, beginning 150 years of conflict. Northampton, recorded in the Anglo-Saxon Chronicle as Hamtune, was held by the Danes from 917 to 921.

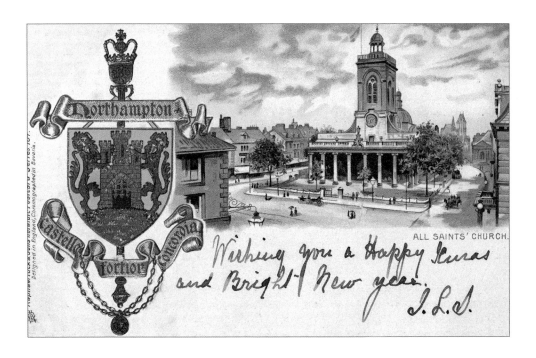

ALL SAINTS' CHURCH.

The settlement was burned out by Sweyn in 1010 and the county ransacked, after which came Canute in 1015 and a brief spell of peace. In 1064 Harold brought an army to the town on behalf of Edward the Confessor to fight Morcar, Earl of Northumbria, and there was more devastation. Eleventh-century life was rarely dull.

William the Conqueror ushered in greater stability and the Domesday Book records the town's name as Northantone, with 295 houses. Military and ecclesiastical aristocracy controlled the land. The homestead or home farm was granted to Simon de Senlis (or St Liz), who became first Earl of Northampton by order of William Rufus, the Conqueror's son. He married William's niece Matilda, built the castle and enlarged the town's defences, while the second Earl established the nunnery at Delapre Abbey. By 1189 there were 300 houses in the town, and its growth would be encouraged by its profitable position in the Nene Valley, at the convergence of lucrative trade routes.

In the early Middle Ages several important parliaments were convened at Northampton, and it became a popular resort of kings. Richard the Lionheart granted the town's charter in his coronation year of 1189 in return for money for the third crusade. The charter was generous, giving townsfolk the right to elect their own reeve – the title changed to mayor in 1215 – and to collect taxes. In brief, it granted the same rights and privileges as those enjoyed by the City of London.

Even before this, Richard's father Henry II had been a frequent visitor, and it was here that he held the fateful council in October 1164 to judge his former friend Thomas Becket, the Archbishop of Canterbury, on charges of 'malfeasance and defiance of the King'. It was this judgment more than any other single factor that provoked the major conflict between church and state that was to blight both men's lives.

The town prospered from the wool and cloth industry, and gained a university. This development offered rich pickings in an age when brute force could secure advantage. During Henry III's reign the town was a centre of piety and learning, with students flocking in from Oxford and Cambridge. Northampton sent two burgesses to the first English parliament. Three orders of friars established themselves, the Franciscans (Grey Friars) in 1224, the Dominicans or friars preachers in around 1230 and the Carmelites (White Friars) in 1271. Later they were followed by the Augustinians or Austin friars.

Local barons supported by students rebelled against the king in 1264; but the monks, then a political breed, undermined the defences and let in the royal force. Pardoned four years later, the town was never quite trusted again – and rightly so, for Northampton turned against the king during the English Civil War. Its disloyalty was not wholly unforgiven, however. When most of the town was razed by fire in 1675 – after a woman in a lane at the end of St Mary Street set her thatched roof alight – Charles II offered help and reduced taxes. Disaster became a blessing, and in 1724 Daniel Defoe described the rebuilt town as the handsomest in this part of England, 'finely rebuilt with brick and stone and the streets spacious and wide'.

There were other troubles. Trade made the town a thoroughfare which brought plague, 'the beggars desease'. In the Black Death which halved England's population in 1348 and '49 Northampton lost, among others, the Master of St John's Hospital, the Prioress of Delapre Abbey and Robert de Holcot, an eminent Dominican friar known as 'the firm and unwearied doctor'. More than seven out of ten of the clergy died. Plague visited again in 1578, between 1603 and '51 and in 1638, each time with devastating effect.

Northampton's last parliament, called on 5 November 1381, levied the notorious poll tax for Richard II, and so helped trigger Wat Tyler's peasant rebellion. The town gained its first charter of incorporation in 1445, entitled 'The Mayor, Bailiffs and Burgesses of Northampton'. The Wars of the Roses threatened renewed upheaval, reaching fields southeast of town on 10 July 1460 in an affray in which Henry VI, who had been lodging at Greyfriars, was captured.

Until 1489 Northampton's government had been 'broad based upon the people's will'. The mayor's need to visit the Barons of the Exchequer in London to be sworn in was ended by a new charter in 1478. The common folk had met in the nave of St Giles' Church to elect the mayor and twelve officials; now parliament decreed the mayor should select the next mayor and bailiffs. All vacancies would now have to be filled in this way, making it a closed corporation until the reforms of 1835.

The Industrial Revolution accelerated the growth of local industries, especially shoe making, which first prospered through using the hides of local animals. These industries and rich farmland also spawned a vigorous blacksmith's trade, which in turn evolved into fairly heavy engineering. By 1712 the town's population was almost 5,000, and most of the workers among them were engaged in shoe-making and hosiery. London's shoe companies were attracted in by comparatively low wages, and the Victorian age saw factories and terraces of tiny houses unfold across the eastern landscape, bringing with them the town's first urban working class.

The Municipal Corporation Act of 1835 created local borough councils. Northampton's burgesses were empowered to elect councillors, and the councillors elected a mayor for one year. Northampton was one of the more important boroughs, and it benefited from more reform in 1888 when it became a county borough responsible for all local government services in its area. In 1864, Godwin's remarkable Guildhall was complete, a most fitting symbol of the town's emerging role, and it was extended by Matthew Holding in 1892. By 1906 the population had reached 92,340.

The economic and social impact of the two world wars was as great in Northampton as in any other part of the country, and the inter-war years were a time of a different kind of hardship; the postwar period has brought new prosperity, but at a cost of social upheaval. The effect of this was powerfully analysed by Jeremy Seabrook, a writer descended from shoe-makers. He recalled in *The Everlasting Feast* (Penguin, 1974) the impression of Northampton Grammar School gained by working-class pupils who were there after passing the eleven-plus: 'We met in the no man's land of those who have rejected their social formation. Our teachers – who seemed to live on a single estate constructed during the 1930s and were consumed with nostalgia for an anti-urban medievalism that strung chains of timbered, gabled homesteads around the town – failed to present us with any good reason for a commitment to any social or intellectual values.' Colin Dunn, a young King's Heath primary teacher in the 1950s, was well aware that: 'Some of our eleven-plus successes found it hard to fit in. The grammar school was a very different social world.'

In fact you did not need to be an intellectual to get by in the '50s. Young people found plenty of factory work, skilled or otherwise; the European Union and all its restrictions and opportunities were a long way off. Cheap foreign competition, especially in the shoe trade, had yet to do its worst. Still, for some, the writing was on the wall. Young ex-serviceman Martin Blane recalled his cobbler's apprenticeship with Bletchley Co-op. He had expected to start his own business, and before the war he would finish work early once a week for his 26-mile bike ride to Northampton College: 'Cycling was far less aggro. A lot of the roads I used have gone. Everyone was in the same boat, less worry, less fear. We were well taught in all aspects of shoe-making, but I could see there was no future in it. So much had changed. People expected much more after the war. Things weren't going to be the same.'

The 1950s saw the last days of the New Theatre, where Martin Blane enjoyed the variety shows, the successors of music hall, and another local man, Gordon Pell, remembers their final throes as nude reviews where naked ladies adopted statuesque poses; they were not allowed to move for the sake of public decency. Soon after that, pop groups would briefly bring new life to the old halls, and crowds of hysterical girls chased after the Beatles at the ABC cinema in 1963.

Gordon White was another young ex-serviceman returning to a different world. He remembers how he and his mates were soon parted from their forces pay-off by the publican, and how hard it was to settle down. Like never before, young people were looking for an outlet, especially after a hard day's work; youth culture was the way forward, and it made money. Soon Abington Street would throng with mini-skirted girls, and shop windows would glow with colour television sets. Youngsters would learn to talk in the national voice of youth. Regional accents would fade or blend with those of the cockney newcomers, more and more of whom were being housed at the government's behest.

16

Grenadier Guards band marching through Abington Street, Northampton, August 1999.

There would be problems, such as what to do with the old folk and how to get people to adapt. These big changes did not make national headlines, but they had their impact. As Jeremy Seabrook commented: 'During 1971 and 1972, the expansion of Northampton became for me a symbol of the new culture, tyrannical and inexorable.'

One remembers a home for unmarried mothers in Harlestone Road in 1967 and the shocking predicament of a girl who found herself in need of such a place. Now Britain has the highest percentage of single mothers in Europe, and planners struggle to accommodate them in communities like Northampton. It is one of the reasons why towns must grow faster. Someone recently wrote to the local paper asking when and where all the development would stop. One shares the wonder. Northampton is an ideal place to soak up apparently endless numbers of people – what with its extensive parkland, the roads and the railways; but the roads, originally planned for speed, are often clogged and under repair – and as for the railways. . . .

So much changed during the 1980s, which some saw as an age of selfishness and greed. Many think the so-called caring '90s are no more magnanimous, but perhaps this brief historical review should end with the optimistic view of Doug Ward, a retired local building director. 'It's all been good steady development,' he says. 'There are always going to be differences of taste and opinion.'

17

A young recruit in the Express Lift light machine shop, 1970s.

Grave New World

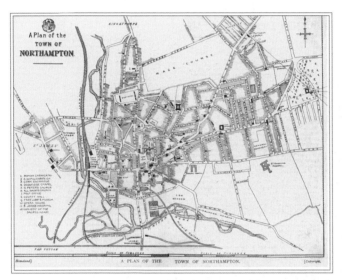

A map of Northampton at around the beginning of a century which brought a new king, the dissolute and self-indulgent Edward VII. Even before the First World War, however, there was change in the air. The nation's working class was organising and the cause of women's emancipation was making ground quickly. This was to be a century of the masses, and of growing uniformity. As yet Northampton still had its peculiarities, its hierarchy of houses, people and shops; but cheap excursions and holidays were helping to put townsfolk in easy touch with a wider world, and the day was fast approaching when the tight-knit boundaries of this map were no longer the limit of their experience.

With many fine families and hotels to service, the Hygienic Laundry, seen here in an advertisement from 1904, was never idle. The practice of laundries and dairies describing themselves as 'hygienic' lasted until well after the Second World War – until it struck them that hygiene should be taken for granted, rather than as a proud boast.

The Pytchley Autocar Co. in Sheep Street, territory out of bounds to all but the richest back in about 1908. Reference to the Royal Automobile Club is a reminder of the days when the motoring organisations were said to exist to warn drivers of police speed traps by their famous salute.

All Saints' Church, *c.* 1903. The building incorporates a statue of Charles II – in Roman attire – in recognition of his giving the town 1,000 tons of timber for rebuilding and halving its taxes for a year after the great fire of 1675. The earlier church on the site – a meeting place for Henry I and English barons during his abortive campaign to win support for his daughter Matilda's claim to the throne – was destroyed by the fire. The current building dates from 1680, and is to a design inspired by Wren. In this century the town's first one-way traffic system went around All Saints' Square, policed in its early days by PC Harry Powell with his stentorian voice.

St Matthew's Church, designed by Matthew Holding, on the tranquil Kettering Road, *c.* 1910. Holding, born in 1846, was a son of Northampton who restored and designed many buildings in the area between 1877 and his death in 1910, several of them in the Gothic style favoured by the Victorians.

The interior of St Matthew's Church, a monument to Matthew Holding's neat and tidy Gothic work.

For a portrait of a fish merchant's, this F. H. Phillips advertisement of 1908 presents as impressive an array of Christmas poultry as you could wish to see. Fish or fowl, the shop's standards of presentation would scarcely please today's public health officials.

Above left: The Northampton Machinery Company factory in Cleveland Road, opened by John Veasey Collier Senior in 1902 to make machines for the increasingly mechanised boot and shoe industry. Encouraged by the demands of the First World War, the company diversified into general engineering and gas engine maintenance.

Above right: John Veasey Collier Senior, Mayor of Northampton in 1937, started his working life managing his father's boot and shoe factory, and it was after inventing several machines for it that he broke away to found the Northampton Machinery Company. His death in the year he was mayor was a huge blow to both the firm and the community.

Right: A frail-looking Rose Sargent, photographed in a studio shortly after she had moved into a house in which the previous tenants, a mother and her four sons, had all died of TB. In those days childbirth was dangerous in itself, but one of several reasons why large families were common was the hope that surviving children would look after their parents in old age.

23

A view from about 1907 of Castle Ashby, stately residence of local power brokers the Comptons, which commands a magnificent view of the Nene Valley. Its walls were fortified by Walter de Langton, Bishop of Coventry, during the time of Edward I, and Sir William Compton bought it during Henry VIII's reign. His grandson Henry was the first Baron Compton, while his eldest son William married Elizabeth, daughter and heiress of the wealthy Sir John Spencer, a Lord Mayor of London. (Judy Ounsworth)

Althorp House, built by Sir John Spencer, who grew rich through sheep in the sixteenth century. The Spencers were descended from the Marlboroughs. The third Baron was created Earl of Sunderland by Charles I; the second Earl excelled in politics and his son Charles, the third Earl, married Anne, daughter of the Duke of Marlborough. The fifth earl became Duke of Marlborough in 1733; Althorp passed to his younger brother John in 1746; and his eldest son was created Viscount and Baron Spencer of Althorp in 1761. That, extremely briefly, is how the present Spencer line began.

The Express Lift Company's Abbey Works, *c.* 1913. Crude elevators were used by Assyrians and ancient Egyptians, but what we would regard as modern lifts began in 1850, driven by steam. The Express Lift Co. was one of two early twentieth-century British companies to specialise in making them. William Stevens founded the other, which moved from London to Northampton in 1909 and as Smith, Major and Stevens built the Abbey Works. Meanwhile, Josiah Easton bought up French patents and prospered with ship hoists and derricks in the First World War. The General Electric Company supplied the power units for Easton's Express Lift Co., and the rival companies each pioneered electric lifts before merging in 1930. GEC bought all the share capital in 1935, and made the company a landmark by building a 418-ft test tower which was opened by the Queen in November 1982. As we note later in the book, the Express Lift Company closed in 1996 – but the tower's impact on the national consciousness was assured when Terry Wogan immortalised it as the Northampton Lighthouse, and for reasons other than its radio fame, it is now a listed building.

Church and Co.'s Duke Street factory shortly after electric motors were installed early this century. This was an important step forward in safety and efficiency for a company which has always prided itself on being ahead of the field.

Shoe-makers in the inter-war years. It was hard and dirty work, performed at high speed. Former shoe-maker Gordon White recalls being asked why he and his mates always left the factory so fast when the whistle blew. 'We're used to doing everything fast,' he replied. 'We have to.'

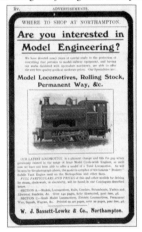

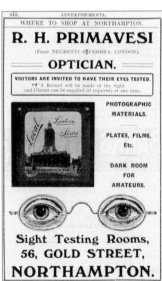

W.J. Bassett-Lowke aimed for 'perfection in miniature', and he succeeded so well that his models were enjoyed by schoolboys and engineers alike. Southampton shipping companies were proud to have his scale replicas in their showcases. He was originally apprenticed to his father's engineering and boilermaking firm, but found international fame in the unusual niche market of miniatures. The factory formerly occupied by his firm is in Kingswell Street.

Mr Primavesi, formerly of Negretti and Zambra of London, projected an exotic air – but his services in eye testing and photographic services must have met practical local needs in Edwardian Northampton.

The view north from the Drapery, *c.* 1895. The trams running along the street would have been horse-drawn at that time, as the Corporation did not start electrifying the system until 1904. The horses, which were stabled at the Ridings, were steadily replaced over the next ten years. By 1934 their electric counterparts had suffered the same fate, superseded by buses.

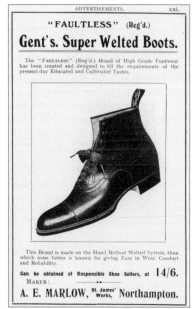

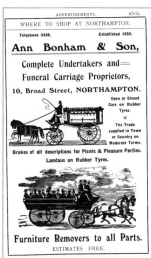

Old cobblers are supposed to have said you could tell the quality of a gent by the cut of his boots. There seems something vaguely raffish about the *Faultless*.

Edwardian Northampton boasted a death rate of 11.6 per 1,000 compared with the national average of 15.4 – but when the inevitable day came, Bonham's could send you off in style. Ann Bonham herself must have been a woman in a thousand when she ventured into business in 1850, a rare achievement for a female in those days.

Abington Street, *c.* 1879. Sadly, the buildings on the right, which housed the Notre Dame School, were demolished in 1979. How wide the boulevard looks; it could almost be Paris! A horse-drawn tram jogs along the centre carriageway, but this was no gentle form of transport. One Saturday in 1902, car number 15, fully loaded, galloped out of control down a crowded Abington Street before overturning on the Wood Hill corner, killing one person and injuring twenty-one.

Left: With its distinctly Dutch-looking gables, Hazelrigg or Cromwell House in Marefair takes its latter name from the tradition that Oliver Cromwell slept here on the eve of the Battle of Naseby in 1645. Thirty years later it escaped the Great Fire. In the eighteenth century the county historian George Baker lived here with his sister, Ann, who wrote a *Northamptonshire Glossary of Words and Phrases. Right*: The Guildhall in about 1907. It was built in 1864 from designs by a 28-year-old Edward Godwin of Bristol; the western extension, designed by Matthew Holding, followed in 1892, and 100 years after that came a further extension by local architects Stimpson, Walton, Bond. Of mainly Gothic style, the front includes statues of monarchs and worthies such as Thomas Becket.

Coronation celebrations for George V in the town centre, with the crowd pressing in on the parading bandsmen, 1910. After his father Edward VII, George turned out to be a dutiful monarch keen to build up the country and the empire, and readily abandoned all his family's German titles to establish his line as the House of Windsor in 1917. Northampton townsfolk always loved a bit of pageantry, but were traditionally wary of royal power.

Excelsior Amateur Athletic Club, 1912. Running was a cheap and accessible sport, popular with working men. Prizes – though never money – could be won at local sports days, and the British Timkens sports ground was a popular venue for many years.

Thomas Sargent, born in Turvey, Bedfordshire, in 1851. His father was a farmworker and had little education. His grandson Gordon White says: 'There was no such thing as childhood then. Tom learned shoe-making at Olney and walked to Northampton to get a job. There he met my gran, Caroline Coleman, and they married at St Edmund's Church.' Tom is pictured in the uniform of the Volunteers, a force similar to the Territorial Army. They had to buy their own uniforms, which were grey with mauve facings.

Laura Sargent, standing on the right, with friends in 1918. Marriage and the right to vote were two major developments soon to change her young life. She worked at Brooke Ladies' Dress Factory in Clarke Road, which has since been replaced by flats.

Dr Doddridge's Academy in Sheep Street, where there is now a commemorative plaque. Philip Doddridge came to town from Kibworth, Leicestershire in 1730 as minister at Castle Hill Independent Church, and he opened his academy for dissenting ministers at the corner of Marefair and Pike Lane before moving to Sheep Street. His other local achievements were a charity school for poor children and an influential role in opening the County Infirmary in George Row, another building which survives as the Northampton and County Club. World-wide, however, he is best known for writing the hymn 'Oh! Happy Day', which was turned into an international hit by the American Edwin Hawkins Singers in 1969. Tuberculosis caused Doddridge's exile to Lisbon in 1751, but he died there almost immediately.

Laura Sargent at a prize giving day at Becket and Sargeant School in Kingswell Street in the early 1900s. She is wearing a gilded oak apple brooch commemorating local affection for Charles II through his gift of timber to the town after the great fire of 1675. Charles sheltered in an oak tree after the Battle of Worcester in 1651, and Oak Apple Day, 29 May, was never more enthusiastically celebrated than in these parts. 'The villages between Northampton and Naseby are the only ones I have come across where most of the children automatically wear oak apples, and defaulters may still be chased out of school,' wrote the social commentator Phyllis Crawford in 1938.

Percy White was one of the first London newcomers to settle in Northampton this century. In the First World War he served with the Royal Army Service Corps and his tasks included collecting cartloads of hay for forage around the Brackley, Towcester and Bicester, assisted by women workers.

Making 'steak and kidney puddings' – shell cases for First World War artillery – at the Express Lift Company's Abbey Works. Women had long made up a fair proportion of Northampton's workforce, but war offered them chances of greater responsibility and more skilled work. Factory safety still had a long way to go, but here the workers wear hats to prevent their long hair from catching in machinery. Other factories such as the Northampton Machine Company were also engaged in war work. On 4 August 1914 the company's founder John Veasey Collier and his father Simon, a shoe manufacturer, were mobilised with the Northamptonshire Yeomanry and both served with distinction in France. Simon, far from a young man, was killed on 14 September 1918. Many women were employed at the machine company in the Second World War, and a number of them became skilled machine tool operators and inspectors.

Today, when many people oppose blood sports, it is easy to forget that hunting was normal for large numbers of rural folk, and a rabbit in the pot could make all the difference to the family's diet. Gun-makers were busy people, and their skills were readily adapted to the demands of the First World War.

Boom and Gloom

The Brooke Ladies' Dress Factory in Clarke Road during the 1930s. It looks rather quaint and is now long gone, replaced by flats. These were uneasy decades between the two world wars. The '20s roared for the rich, and farther down the social scale, ex-servicemen tramped towards relatively prosperous Northampton. High fashion reflected women's newly won emancipation by making their figures appear flat and boyish, while the tight cloche hat became an almost universal accessory. Local woman Margaret Drinkwater recalls: 'We used make-up, but not like today. Just a sort of coloured cream and a bit of lipstick. We had to put that on after we'd gone out – and make sure it was off before we went home.'

Express Lifts' annual carnival parade entering Abbey Works, *c.* 1920. All big companies promoted social activities and summer relaxation. In his book *The Everlasting Feast* the Northampton-born writer Jeremy Seabrook contrasted today's rich with those of the past, saying that today's breed have no sense of guilt or concern for poorer people. Developments in the 25 years since he expressed those views can scarcely have prompted him to revise them.

The Lake, Abington Park, about 1922. Northampton is rich in parkland, and has been more so. In the 1930s, the old racecourse was the main open space and sports ground, with 118.5 acres. Becket's Park, rolling beautifully towards the River Nene, was known affectionately as Cow Meadow and later Midsummer Meadow. This view of Abington Park projects a sense of the peace and calm such open spaces can provide.

Gold Street – named after the goldsmiths who once worked here – delightfully free of traffic congestion but with the odd familiar name prominent, soon after the First World War.

Shoe-makers from Crockett & James on their annual day out to Deanshanger, *c.* 1920. In the 1850s Henry Mayhew wrote: 'The boot and shoe makers are certainly far from being an intellectual body of men. They appear to be a stern, uncompromising and reflective race. This is perhaps to be accounted for by the solitude of their employment.' A different slant on them came from an observer in 1869: 'A large proportion of Northampton shoe makers struck me as being of the alcoholic persuasion.'

The Drapery, Northampton.

The bustling Drapery in about 1919, more than two decades on from the scene on page 27. The area was originally known as the Glovery, and has had a long association with the cloth industry. Margaret Drinkwater recalls riding from Far Cotton into the Drapery on 'graceful trams': 'As a child, I was fascinated by the tram bell. It was different to any other; but trams were a nuisance when I started biking. You could get stuck in the lines.' There was mayhem in 1926 when Mr Cameron, the tramways manager, thought he would help beat the General Strike by driving a tramcar up to the junction with Mercers Row. A crowd of strikers tried to remove all the passengers, but the police made a baton charge and arrested their leaders.

Not quite the Ritz: the Gasometer pub at the junction of Gas Street and Horshoe Street, one of scores of backstreet beerhouses. The First World War had finished, jobs were scarce and men tramped miles to find them, frequently taking refuge in the workhouse. It is easy to see how beer offered some comfort. 'They used to say there was only one town comparable for pubs – and that was Great Yarmouth, where most Northampton folk went for their holidays,' says Gordon White. The area around the Gasometer was demolished and replaced by St Peter's Way.

A Northampton Town & County Building Society advertisement from May 1935, when the company's service was local and personal, though aimed strictly at middle-class buyers. The £1 million of the company's funds available for mortgages would not go very far today, but an interest rate of 4.5 per cent seems attractive enough. The plain truth in 1935 was that for the vast majority of young couples starting out on married life, renting was the only option.

Northampton's first railway station was opened in 1845 at Cotton End, and connected with the main west coast line at Blisworth, four miles away. This picture shows platelayers Albert Powell, R. Gutteridge and Boscoe Taylor at Blisworth in about 1920. Albert's son Baden says: 'They reckon you could tell the time of day by the position of the peak on Boscoe's cap. Dad worked on the railway from 1900 to 1945. He smelled of the wood pickle they used to preserve the sleepers, and creosote, which they used on the keys, the wooden wedges used to hold the lines. They walked the line checking it ten hours a day, then dad did his allotment when he came home. That was like an extra bit of money.'

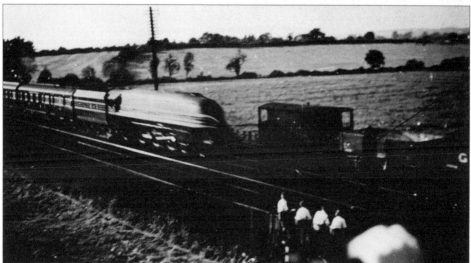

Gordon White and his classmates admire the London Midland & Scottish Railway's Coronation Scot train as it streaks through Blisworth in 1937, most probably hauled by the locomotive Coronation. Streamlining was the big craze of the late '30s, in cars and aircraft as well as engines, and there was huge rivalry between the LMS and the London & North Eastern Railway to provide the fastest and most glamorous route to Scotland. The LNER claimed the glory in 1938 when its Mallard reached 126 mph, a steam loco record, though some sceptics say this was a blip, recorded momentarily when the train was thundering down a steep incline. For sheer class, however, and regular speeds of up to 114 mph, it was hard to match the Coronation Scot, named in celebration of the new King George VI and resplendent in blue livery with a silver stripe all the way back to the guard's van.

Gordon White and his classmates by Blisworth railway bridge with their teacher 'Slasher' Harris after watching the Coronation Scot roar past. Mr Harris earned his nickname because of his way of flourishing the cane, though by the standards of the day it was acknowledged that he never used it without good reason. Blisworth was a popular venue for picnickers who came to watch the expresses going through their paces. In 1838 Stephenson's main line bypassed Northampton because the engines were not powerful enough to climb out of the Nene Valley – and because local landowners did not much want them there, anyway. By 1845, however, the *Northampton Mercury* insisted that: 'The town which has not a railway in its vicinity is an exception, isolated, shut out from the rest of the world.'

Gordon White and his father in Harlestone Woods on the Althorp estate, *c.* 1933. Gordon says: 'It was a good place to go for a day out. In the holidays, if we went anywhere, it was to visit family or friends.' At least there was good cycling country around town, and the chance of the odd rail trip to Skegness, and some older readers might think Jeremy Seabrook was being a little over-gloomy about their childhood years when he wrote: 'Children were born for the boot and shoe trade, casually employed and sacked for drinking or singing. There was no room for ambition. Children copied their parents and heeded adults. They laboured for treasures like a Windsor chair, a cord sofa, vase or gas stove.'

Jim Drinkwater, second left, on a tar wagon during the 1930s, when jobs were scarce. He recalls: 'We were tar spraying the roads around Brixworth way. We lodged there. I was sixteen. We had a horse-pulled tank, and there was fire under this tank which heated the tar. There was a tap, and two chaps had cans which they filled and poured on the road. One day one man fell into the tub, and had to be rushed to hospital. When our old cart-horse had to be shod, I rode it to Market Harborough and back. We used to lose wet time – and we had a lot of rain that year.'

Jim Drinkwater, born just outside town in Heyford, seen at Weedon School, winning first prize in the fancy dress as a rag and bone man. He remembers seeing the old tramps who used to sleep under hedges and in haystacks: 'They never bothered you except perhaps coming to your door for a cup of hot water. Same with gypsies, never did any damage like they do now.'

41

The basic chassis of this bus from the 1930s was an AEC Renown six-wheeler, but the somewhat eccentric bodywork was made locally by Grose of Marefair. Carrying 54 seated passengers, it had the registration number VV 119 and was number 40 in the Northampton Corporation fleet. Later sold to Wesley Bros, it ended its days as a café in St Albans. In fact Grose had a good name for quality coachbuilding, as did their local rivals Mulliners, who displayed cars with their splendid bodies in showrooms near the Plough Hotel. There was great excitement one year when they shipped out a car to a fabulously rich Indian Rajah.

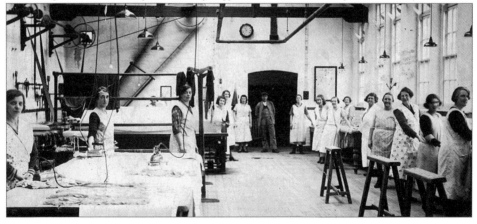

Northampton General Hospital laundry in the early 1930s, where Becky Pacey, the grandmother of the owner of this photograph, Pam Reynolds, was one of the workers. It was an industrious team, but not all memories of the hospital are of spotless cleanliness. 'I remember this ward with high distempered walls,' recalled Colin Dunn, who was in for three weeks as a child. 'You could see a mark about two feet from the ceiling, where they couldn't reach beyond step-ladder height.'

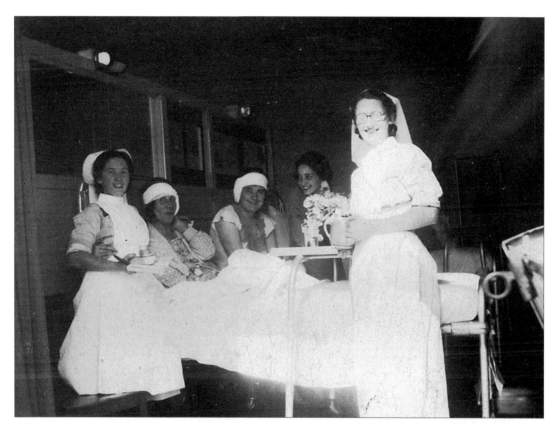

Ear operation patients and their nurses at Northampton General Hospital, 1930s. One of the patients is Kathleen Pacey, who coincidentally worked at the hospital. Colin Dunn, in hospital as a 13-year-old, recalls Friday mornings, when the great billowing 'Cutty Sark' figure of the matron would lead god-like specialist doctors into immaculately prepared wards, and they would poke and prod patients who would be too scared to argue, complain or even discuss their ailments. Another local resident, Margaret Drinkwater, remembers having to pay for the doctor: 'You'd send the bill to the sick club, usually about five bob. The old nurse would come out if you were having a baby. You could give her something, but she'd do it for nothing.'

Fred Coles, mid-1930s. He recalls it being the done thing for families to own a piano, 'so when mother bought it she decided one of us would have to play it. I started aged seven, practising in the front room half an hour an evening and improving slightly, while my mates came knocking on the window, waving cricket bats for a game at the racecourse. So mother compromised and I did it mornings instead. Then accordions came in fashion. I came second in the open solo championships of the Midlands in 1938.'

The Ambassadors Dance Band, late 1930s. Fred Coles was a founder member and says: 'I became quite proficient and did quite a bit of charity work. I played at some high class clubs, but I started thinking I should go where I could earn a few bob. I was fourteen or fifteen when I first played at dances on piano, along with a fiddle and drums. Then I was with Ted Adams in an accordion band, playing five nights a week for half a crown an hour for three hours.' It was a useful supplement to his day job at that time in the shoe factory.

The Ambassadors in the mood for something completely different. Fred Coles had left Ted Adams and the accordion band to join the Ambassadors when they were still the Carlton Players, a five-piece dance band. The new name brought an increase in personnel, and the band was enterprising enough to hire the Exeter Hall and run its own dances there. 'Girlfriends came along,' Fred recalls. 'At first we played like hell and got nowhere, but at the end we were getting three hundred people in, stacking them on each other's shoulders and making £3 a night. We felt we had to keep pushing new things, and this picture shows one of our crazy nights.' The band started in 1937 and lasted through to the beginning of the Second World War.

Local men Roy Gardner and Gordon White were quick to answer the call to arms in 1939. 'When war started, I had little chance of becoming aircrew because my education was limited,' Gordon recalls. 'I had always been interested in planes, and had followed the adventures of Amy Johnson, Scott and Black. I wanted to be a flier, so with a pal I joined the ATC, then the Air Defence Force Corps. We used an old factory in Portland Street, and were kitted out in RAF uniforms. We had lectures every evening and general parades on Thursday nights. They paid for our evening classes on subjects such as maths at Northampton College in George's Avenue. I volunteered for aircrew and went to Cardington for attestation on maths and physical fitness. Of course, we all wanted to be pilots – but I settled for wireless operator/gunner.'

Doris Ward in 1939. Her mother died when she was two. She was the youngest of seven children and her father brought them up, in spite of pressure to put some of them in homes. It was tough, but there were some happy times: 'We used to sit in the front room and he'd play the pianola.'

Doris's husband-to-be Doug Ward in the early 1930s at a Scout camp near Gosport, Hampshire. Doug says: 'I always had a fancy to join the Navy. I liked to get down to Portsmouth to see the ships. I saw the war as an opportunity, and volunteered.'

War Once More

Local sailors Doug Ward (right) and John Callow respond to a call from the legendary *Chronicle* photographer Roland Holloway to deliver a splash of naval colour to a patriotic gathering while on leave in November 1941. The speaker between them was an admiral. Remarkably, the only serious wartime incident in Northampton was when a stricken Stirling bomber crashed at night in July 1941. Jim Drinkwater was out calling up train crews for duty: 'The ammunition was still going off when I got there. They'd closed it off. I was at the top off Bridge Street. There was quite a fire and you didn't want to get too close. The crew had baled out.'

Margaret Drinkwater recalls the bugbears of food shortage and clothes rationing: 'There was a man on the market who'd sell you something nice for extra cash. There were always big boys making money. I could buy a dress for 5 shillings. We didn't have nylons, they were sort of silk. Americans brought the nylons, though there weren't many of them in town. For jellies I bought gelatine from the chemist and pure fruit juice to flavour it. I was doing that one night when a doodlebug came over the rooms we rented in Parkfield Avenue. We went upstairs with the children and didn't know what to do.'

Her husband Jim recalls the Italian prisoners of war: 'They used to come in our loco shed cleaning engines. Give 'em a two-shilling piece and they'd make a beautiful bracelet. They weren't that different, except they spoke Italian if they didn't want you to understand. Some stayed and married local girls.'

After the war, Britain was virtually bankrupt and hard work and rationing continued. Northampton had the resources and willpower to do its bit. Fred Coles became a tool-maker after returning from a Japanese PoW camp. He recalled a comrade there saying: 'We'll never survive.' He replied: 'You may not, but I will.' It spoke volumes for his town's gritty spirit. Like the nation, Northampton would eventually move from gloom to boom.

J.V. Collier Jnr leading the Duke of Gloucester on a tour of the Northampton Machinery Company's works during the Second World War, when it diversified spectacularly from shoe making equipment to produce small arms ammunition machinery, machine tools and specialist tools for making submarine detection gear.

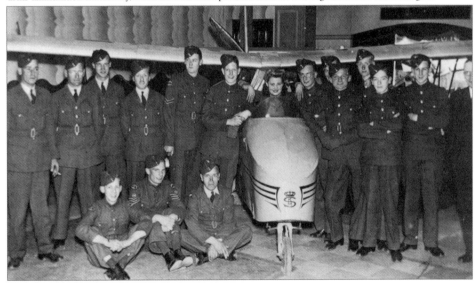

Northampton ATC at the Exchange cinema in 1942, before watching *A Yank in the RAF*, starring Tyrone Power. The girl in the sail plane is an usherette, and the cinema manager is on the far right, next to Peter Rideout. When Peter was demobbed from the Navy in Australia he joined the Royal Australian Air Force and settled Down Under.

A superb picture of young evacuees arriving from London at Castle station, August 1941. The move was a culture shock for many who came from areas of poverty and hardship. Schools were placed under strain and in some cases a shift system was needed. The singing Beverley Sisters were among those who flocked to Northampton as youngsters.

In the RAF at last, Gordon White is all dressed up with somewhere to go; no doubt he especially appreciated the fine quality flying boots. He remembers how difficult it was to settle back into life in civvy street in Northampton: 'My father was teetotal and my mother drank only at parties, but I drank regularly when I got overseas. Shorts were as cheap as beer, if not cheaper. When I came home I went out with my pals to pubs in the town centre like the Lord Palmerston, where there's a burger bar now. We had our forces gratuities in our hands and couldn't wait to hand them over to the brewers.'

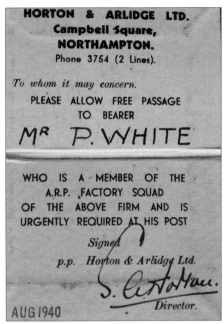

HORTON & ARLIDGE LTD.
Campbell Square,
NORTHAMPTON.
Phone 3754 (2 Lines).

To whom it may concern.
PLEASE ALLOW FREE PASSAGE
TO BEARER
Mʀ P. WHITE

WHO IS A MEMBER OF THE
A.R.P. FACTORY SQUAD
OF THE ABOVE FIRM AND IS
URGENTLY REQUIRED AT HIS POST
Signed
p.p. Horton & Arlidge Ltd.

AUG 1940   *Director.*

Left: Bryan Douglas, who volunteered for aircrew on his eighteenth birthday and was soon passed A1.
Right: Red tape: this is a pass for a member of the Air Raid Precautions squad at Horton and
Arlidge's box and packaging factory in Campbell Square – to be shown to the authorities if he had to
rush there in an emergency.

Left: Audrey Banks, Land Army girl at work on Moulton Park Farm. Bryan Douglas recalls her as a
girl visiting a mutual friend next door in Park Avenue North. he had always thought of her as
someone special, and when he was invited round to play tennis, the pair hit it off! *Right:* Audrey
Banks getting to grips with real horse power on Moulton Park Farm. Land Army girls often came
from a very different world from the men they were helping, but before long most of them more than
pulled their weight.

The Air Minister reviews cadets at Sywell Aerodrome, 1941. Bryan Douglas found himself in a controlled occupation at Express Lifts in the early part of the war, but used his family's old business address in Wellingborough to apply for the RAF. He eventually made it in May 1941 – but the fact that he passed out one of the top two in his flight meant being kept away from the action for longer than he liked, as an instructor in Canada.

Bryan Douglas and fellow RAF instructors at Sywell, 1945. They were great fliers and there was a fine spirit among them, but many of them envied their colleagues at the sharp end of operations.

By 1944 Bryan Douglas was back in England and getting used to flying in British weather, having luckily been transferred to No. 6 EFTS at Sywell, just five miles from home. The picture shows his wedding to Audrey Banks in March 1944.

Doug and Doris Ward on their wartime wedding day. Leading seaman Gordon Midgeley was best man and Doris's sister Connie was matron of honour. Doug and Doris used to see one another when he was an apprentice decorator pushing his cart and she was going the other way to the shoe factory: 'We first spoke at the Picturedrome in Kettering Road. She was wearing a big silly hat, sitting in front of me. I said: "Would you mind taking it off?" She said: "No, I won't." It grew from there!'

Fred and Hettie Coles just after war ended – a hard war. Fred recalls: 'At first I was in the Northants Regiment, but we were decimated at Dunkirk. I was then drafted into the Norfolks and captured by the Japanese. Working near the Burma border, I had a tropical ulcer on my right leg and a hole in it, so I started trading what valuables I had hidden for extra food. When I was up on the highest point on the railway they sent me and the rest of the seriously sick back down the river, to base camp on a barge. The trip took a week. Maggots crawling out from under the dressing worried me, but the medics said: "They only eat bad meat. They'll clean the wound." My music came in handy. I had Aussie orderlies washing my wound with salt water, and one of them said if I could teach him music, he'd do me an extra dressing. That may have been what did the trick and healed it.'

Jim Drinkwater's Vincent HRD Comet motorbike in 1949, one of thirteen he has owned: 'I've never driven a car. I bought that Vincent from a bloke in London. He rode it down and I gave him his dinner, his fare back and £15. I'd get £5,000 for it if I had it today.' Of his driving test, Jim recalls: 'It was snowing enough to blind you. There were four examiners round the circuit. They jumped out in front of you for the emergency stop. I came back the wrong way down Billing Road, but they still passed me. There weren't many one-way systems then.'

An ERF four-wheeler lorry belonging to C. Butt in the late '40s – fitted with a Cummings diesel engine after Gerald Butt had been impressed by the robust power units the company supplied for Euclid dumper trucks. Today Butt's still run a few ERFs, but Volvos are the backbone of their 200-strong fleet.

Ex-servicemen on a course at Northampton College, learning how to make shoes by hand. It was not long before many of them decided that their future lay elsewhere in postwar Britain. On the back row, far left, is instructor Fred Bending, with Bill McGurk and Gordon White – who did stay in shoe-making – next to him.

Gwen, Susan and Bob Wesley and John Maloney with an AEC Regent at their terminus in the Mayorhold, late 1940s. The next bus along is a Leyland Tiger. These were the kind of workhorses that gave so many Northampton people a glimpse of the wider world in the years after the war.

The dream was 'Homes fit for Heroes', but the reality for many young families after the war was an aluminium prefab like this one at Drayton Kingsthorpe. They were supposed to last ten years. In fact this picture is from 1969, shortly before the one seen here was demolished. Rare examples still survive in some parts of the country – some as listed buildings!

Gordon White riding his motorcyle in the years after the war. The fact that it is a German NSU speaks of a world getting back to normal, though it would be a long time before some other Britons would readily accept German or Japanese goods. Easing his way back into civilian life after the war, Gordon found touring on his motorbike a great release from the shoe factory.

From Gloom to Boom

Express Lifts workmen enjoying simple pleasures, early 1950s style. Rationing was on the wane but exports still took priority and luxuries were few. The Festival of Britain in 1951 made a bold statement about the future, but in real life Britain was still heavily in debt to the United States, and its commitment to the remains of its Empire meant that easy overseas markets had to be abandoned. Railways and hospitals were nationalised after Labour's landslide victory in 1946; but the return of the Conservatives put haulage back into hands of private operators such as Northampton's William Butt, and the '50s became a time of under-investment in railways and the rise of motor transport.

Local man Jim Drinkwater recalls a time when his brother owned one of only three cars in the village of Heyford. By 1959, Britain's first motorway of any great length, the M1, swept past Northampton's outskirts, and it was only a matter of time before thousands of London's overspill population came with it, refugees from war damage, land speculation and the decay of Victorian housing. Northampton was still very rural in 1951; the cattle market handled 171,989 animals that year. The planners clearly believed that moving people to the country was the answer to all urban ills.

Good times were coming slowly. In 1959 the Conservative Prime Minister Harold Macmillan went to the country asserting: 'You've never had it so good.' Northampton folk were not so sure, and rejected the Tory glamour girl Jill Knight in favour of the Labour stalwart R.T. Paget. His party offered 'a white hot technological revolution', but it was a good old sex scandal – the Profumo affair – that probably did most to put the Tories out of office in 1964. Nearer to home, Northampton had much of which to be proud: sound achievements through the 1944 Education Act, not least a fine college of technology, plus all-round sterling efforts in public service.

Left: A New Theatre programme for the D'Oyly Carte Opera's production of *The Mikado* in April 1950. The metropolitan view of the D'Oyly Carte was that its monopoly on professional Gilbert and Sullivan had made it dull and stale, but its visits to Northampton were always well enjoyed. The New Theatre was a variety venue. 'Comics, jugglers, singers, they could go round using the same acts for years,' local man Martin Blane recalls. 'Now television means they have to come up with new material every week.'

Frank Dobson's statue *Woman with Fish* shortly after its unveiling in Memorial Square in May 1952. Modern art was something that many people did not understand, and it is hard today to understand the anger it aroused in its opponents. Whatever the reason, it was daubed with paint and the head was knocked off; repaired, and after a period in hiding, it was unveiled again in the wilds of Delapre Park.

Express Lift staff prepare to board their luxury coach for an away bowling match in about 1953. Northampton's first motor bus services started in 1923, soon rivalling trams, offering flexibility and extending the limits of public transport.

An ERF Cummings diesel engine powered eight-wheeler, part of Butt's up-to-the-minute fleet in the 1950s.

Haulage contractor Gerald Butt at his desk in 1991. Behind him is a painting of his company's founder, Charles Butt, a well-built man who joined the Army under-age and became one of its boxing champions. After an apprenticeship and National Service, Gerald started work for the family firm in its workshops. He says Northampton's central position in the country has aided the company's growth in road haulage.

At Wilson Plant Hire's Weedon Road depot in 1958, a C. Butt Scammell Highwayman and low loader prepare to take out a Priestman Wolf shovel for quarrying work. Quarries have been an important part of the local economy for many years.

The Express Lift Company offices in the early 1950s. Today, one small machine can do the work of this number of assiduous clerical staff.

The Express Lift Company's Abbey Works at South Bay, April 1950. The company was a world leader in supplying controlled lifts, but that counted for nothing in 1996 when, shortly after GEC sold out to the American giant Otis, the new parent company announced its closure.

Express Lift Company firemen at the firm's 1953 sports day. Other organisations also had their own private brigades, including British Timken and St Crispin's Hospital. On many occasions these firefighters turned out for blazes that would otherwise have had to wait for the public fire brigade.

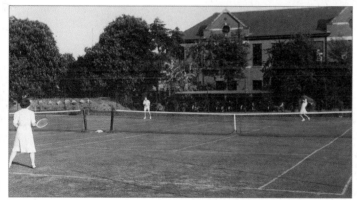

Tennis late 1950s style on the Express Lift courts. They were a fine facility, but economics rule, and in the '80s they were turned into a visitors' car park. Now economics have ruled again, and the company itself has gone.

Late 1950s, and St John's Street station is boarded up long before Dr Richard Beeching's axe fell, having closed in the summer before war broke out in 1939. After that, Bedford and Wellingborough passengers had to use Castle or Bridge Street stations.

Coronation celebrations in Northumbria Gardens, Abington, 1953. This was to be the dawn of a new Elizabethan age that would see the last days of Empire and much more upheaval besides – a good deal of it affecting the royal family itself.

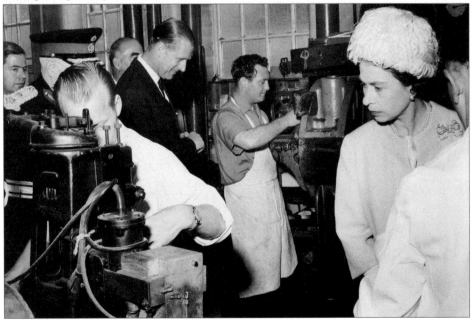

The Queen visiting Church's St James factory in July 1965 apparently unperturbed by the strong tang of glue and leather and the steady murmur of machinery. Prince Philip shows equal interest in the background.

J.V. Collier Jnr, Mayor of Northampton, at a celebratory reception given by his Northampton Machinery Company for 200 employees at the Whyte Melville Hall in Fish Street, May 1954. They were still austere days, and the main meal consisted of cold ham and tongue; but they were also days of optimism as the party toasted the young Queen, and when the new Mayor described his first engagement as a wonderful climax to his first day in office was cheered enthusiastically by his workers. 'I talked in the council chamber of the family firm,' he told them. 'Can I ask you not to think this means a lot of tripe? It is worth a lot these days when the whole structure of life is getting less personal.' Mr Collier was a leading member of the local Conservative Party, but his son Simon fears he would not have liked all that has happened in the town since his time: 'There was terrific potential for change in the 1960s, and they had a great town to start with. They could have made a feature of the river between St Andrews and Bedford Road, for instance. Some lovely old buildings disappeared, like the Peacock Hotel. There wasn't enough thought, it all happened too quickly.' Today the Northampton Machinery Company concentrates on making cable winding equipment.

Jim Drinkwater in the back yard of his home in St Leonard's Road, Far Cotton, in 1958, just back from a shift on the railways and reunited with one of his beloved motorbikes. He drove steam locos, but said there were no special ceremonies when they were phased out: 'Most of them just went to the scrapyard at Kettering.'

The successful 1959 football team at King's Heath School, which served one of the town's major postwar estates. Colin Dunn, the teacher second from the right, recalls the boys as being tough but likeable. 'In PE I liked to show off, racing those eleven-year-olds, until one day I didn't beat them. One of them said: "Sir, it's the smoking." I said: "Right, I'll stop." "Bet you can't," they said – but I haven't touched a cigarette since.'

Every major company fielded a cricket team until life grew earnest. This is Express Lift's office and works club at the beginning of the 1952 season. There was great rivalry between Express and the team at British Timken, which also enjoyed the facilities of a fine ground.

One of Northamptonshire Grammar School's junior rugby XVs in around 1958. Boys then were addressed by their surnames, so in that tradition: back row, Robinson and Brind; second row, Manning, Robinson, Jeffries, Tarpley, Barrit, Stapleton; front row, Mason, Hull, O'Brien, Taylor, Gardiner, Soames. Traditionally, the grammar school was a good source of supply for the town's Saints rugby team, now a formidable force in English rugby.

The Northampton Machinery Company workshop seen in the early 1950s, during its transition from producing boot and shoe making equipment to cable winding.

Simon Collier with his mother at the NMC Christmas party at the Salon de Danse, Franklin's Gardens, 1957. It would not be many years before full responsibility for running the company fell on his shoulders, but in the meantime he had to face the music and dance. The Gardens were named after John Campbell Franklin, who bought them in 1886. He later sold out to a company which extended into the old Abbey Gardens, adding a sports ground, cycling track and bandstand.

More happy sporting memories long gone. Express Lifts kept an immaculate bowling green, and here a veteran player demonstrates the art to youngsters at the company's sports day in 1951.

Two boys having fun with a pot of bubbles in the 1950s. Here's hoping that these lads' dreams, unlike those in the 'Bubbles' song, did not fade and die.

A King's Heath performance of John Masefield's 'Cargoes'. Former teacher Colin Dunn remembers a headteacher there, Stan Hutchins: 'One boy caused a lot of trouble, and was punished. His mother came in furious, saying: "You can't teach me anything about children, I've brought up seven." The head replied: "Madam, you breed them, I bring them up!"'

A nativity play by class 4b at King's Heath, 1957. Doubtless the children were not always as angelic as they appear here.

Express Lift employees taking refreshments at the Fox and Hounds, Harlestone, in the summer of 1955, when car ownership was still only for the comfortably-off. More senior staff had been competing in a company car rally, a popular relaxation on the comparatively uncluttered country roads of that time.

Left and below: Fun – and what looks like some serious fund-raising – at the Express Lift Company fete, 1952. The girl on the left of the group of women proudly displays her Notre Dame school blazer.

Bob Wesley's Seddon coach at Silverstone, home of the British Grand Prix, in the mid-1950s. There was a time when life on the circuit was a great deal more laid-back than it is now. Local man Doug Ward bought a 1930 Austin Seven after the Second World War for £15, taught himself to drive, and took his son out for a spin on the Silverstone track one Sunday afternoon: 'We just drove on, but I went at no great speed.'

The dashing Peter Collins in his 2.5 litre Ferrari V6 setting a new Silverstone lap record of more than 105 mph while beating Roy Salvadori's Cooper in the *Daily Express* International Trophy race of May 1958. Shortly afterwards, Collins was killed at the German Grand Prix.

Pamela Reynolds, then Pacey, outside Mounts Swimming Baths at the age of fourteen in 1957. Fashion consciousness was reaching an ever-younger market in the late 1950s, and social commentators were beginning to take great interest in teenage spending power. Sedate stars such as the Beverley Sisters who had visited in the '50s – they are still performing today, incidentally, though unashamedly a great deal less sedately – were replaced in the early '60s by the Beatles and their many imitators; and with them came all the trappings of modern youth culture.

Errol Flynn, who was once in rep. at the Royal Theatre, returned to town in the '50s and met some of the theatre's current crop of actors. A one-time Benny Hill stooge, Henry McGee, is directly above the star, who as ever is performing the lady's man routine. Errol had a reputation for chasing the girls around the corridors of the Royal; and, indeed, on reflection, around every other room of every other building he ever visited.

Wesley's booking office, late 1950s. Bob Wesley pioneered continental coach tours after the war, with the advertisement on the door reminding customers that it was time to be seeing Germany in a different light. They also organised trips rather closer to home, as Bob's wife Gwen recalled: 'We used to take schoolchildren to Olney. I went on the bus and kept them in order. They hated me.'

The Singing Sixties

The picture shows what remains of H. Brain's shoe repair shop in Bridge Street in the early 1960s. Fly posters advertise a shocking new band, the Rolling Stones. Times were ripe for postwar baby boomers to revolt against all the virtuous aspirations war-weary parents had had for them. Hemlines went up, dance clubs opened and teenage pregnancies rocketed. It was a free-and-easy lifestyle to which authority and older people in general found it hard to adapt. A young mother from those days recalls: 'I was in a home for unmarried mothers in Harlestone Road. Northampton was like the big city. We were allowed into town, and I remember going to Brierleys, but they didn't like us seeing men. I was told off for talking to the gardener. They weren't keen on us keeping our babies, and half of them were adopted.'

So much of the old was coming down. Northampton Development Corporation was set up in 1968, with 281,000 acres set aside for the population to reach 230,000 by 1981. People had to react quickly to decisions from on high – from planners, politicians and businessmen. Even the rebellious teenagers were dancing to big business's tune, but it seemed fun, and freedom at last. Labour returned to power in October 1964, offering a new order, but many of the old problems remained. It was an excellent backcloth for an angst-ridden television industry and angry playwrights; but in many ways, Northampton was its own theatre – and there were about to be many changes of scene.

Claremont and Belmont flats viewed from derelict buildings, 1964. Pictures such as this aimed to symbolise modern progress, but three decades on it is widely accepted that high-rise flats were not the solution to the housing needs of the postwar years.

Suzanne Rollestone pictured in the back yard of her home at Marefair sub-post office and newsagents in 1961, wearing her first Notre Dame school uniform – a serge dress with detachable primrose yellow collar and cuffs. It was expensive and could only be dry cleaned, and many families breathed a sigh of relief when the school changed to normal skirts and blouses. Notre Dame was run by a French order of nuns for Catholic girls in the area plus a few assisted places.

The view from the bus stop in Harborough road in March 1964, a scene of ageing buildings and open space typical of the time when the town had done away with so much of the old and had not yet replaced it with the new.

The girls of Notre Dame school wore split shifts and bloomers for PE, apparently modelled on the garb of ancient Greece. Bridget Hickey, on the far right, seems to have taken the image to heart and struck a classical pose. The other girls, from left to right, are Barbara Buckley, Geraldine Mackenzie and Vicky Finnis, with Diana Urquhart in front. They are pictured in the peaceful and relaxing school gardens at the end of summer term in 1965. A developer bought Notre Dame and the whole site was bulldozed one Sunday in 1979. People protested that it should have been listed, but they were too late; they were told the space was needed for shops and offices.

Spring Lane Primary School sports day, *c.* 1964. Proud parents Eric and Kathleen Rollestone are at the winning tape applauding the efforts of their younger daughter Judith. Now a lawyer working in London, she has come a long way from the snug terraces that used to be part of a self-policing community.

People lived here, once: the way is being cleared for a new road project from Harding Street to Monks Pond Street in April 1962.

A crowd gathers at Becket's Park to watch the carnival parade in 1962. Local poet Dominic Allard is toward the left. Commenting on the changes in town, he wrote: 'I recalled the bleakness that followed when the demolition workers had finished. There were streets of rubble where houses used to be.' In his poem 'Clearance Area' he mused: Who can say now/that anything was here,/other than open land,/used only by stray dogs.

Suzanne Rollestone in the back yard of her home at Marefair sub-post office and newsagents, *c.* 1963. She is holding her kitten Moses and longing for the countryside and house with big garden from which her family had recently moved. Now the view from the family shop's yard was of Hamp's furniture warehouse in Freeschool Street.

A Thames Trader lorry belonging to a local coal merchant in the Mayorhold, April 1962. With many people moving into centrally heated flats, the coalman's business was starting to decline. Coalmen humping hundredweight sacks of coal on their backs were a common sight into the 1960s, as was a dwindling number of tradesmen's horse-drawn carts. Dominic Allard reckons his father's scrap metal cart was the last horse-drawn vehicle used regularly on Northampton streets.

King's Heath School visits the Grand Union Canal near Milton Malsor, *c.* 1962. No doubt the children were learning of the times when the canals were built and about when, in 1763, the Lords Halifax and Northampton gave money to schemes to make the River Nene navigable to vessels carrying cheap imported fuel. The next step was a connecting branch of the Grand Union Canal via a 3,076 yard tunnel from Blisworth. It opened in 1805 and took five years to build, since the first attempts to tunnel had failed due to flooding. The building of the Blisworth tunnel brought Northampton's first stretch of railway line in 1800, connecting the sections of canal on either side of the excavation work. Of course it was railways that eclipsed canals in the middle of the last century, but the leisure use of inland waterways has grown in recent years.

Jim and Margaret Drinkwater on a motorbike outing to their home village of Heyford in the late 1950s. Jim has vivid memories of riding his bike a decade or so later: 'Ten yards from home, I looked up and saw the new Concorde, hit the kerb and fell off. Everyone saw it and laughed.'

An old Commer two-stroke lorry abandoned on derelict land off Church Lane, August 1963. The town already had its first three-storey flats at St Katharine's Court in the old Boroughs, where there had previously been close-knit streets.

Modern flats in the background and Johnson's dark blue and grey Strachan Ford bus at the Mayorhold bus station, October 1968. All the independent bus companies pulled in here, while the National Bus subsidiary United Counties had its own station at Derngate.

The Drapery, looking north, 1969. The handcart and ladders on the left are a quaint touch, but their time is all but past. The street used to be a focal point of local life, a place where you always saw someone you knew, and older local people see today's national high street chain stores as a step backwards from the characterful shops of old. The late Dr W. E. Brocklehurst remembered working at chemists Philadelphus Jeyes: 'There were vaults under the road where orange wine settled and matured before being used in Quinine and Orange Wine Tonic. We produced everything from sterile injections to conditioning powder for horses and ointment for foot-rot in sheep.'

Eric Rollestone outside his Marefair sub-post office and newsagents, c. 1967. His daughter Suzanne worked hard helping him, marking up the papers for delivery. 'There was quite a community living over the shops in Marefair,' she recalled. 'Not just locally born people, Greek Cypriots and all sorts. New property rates killed all that.'

The modest frontage of Northampton Royal Theatre in July 1964, before redevelopment linked it with the Derngate Centre. The town's first recorded performers were Mr Jones's company of comedians from London, who opened in June 1742. The original Royal was in Northampton's first gas-lit building, tiny premises on the corner of Marefair and Horseshoe Street in 1824. John Franklin, hotelier and owner of Franklin's Gardens in St James, commissioned the building seen here, which was designed by the leading theatre architect Charles John Phipps and opened with *Twelfth Night* in May 1884. Complete with stage and stalls underground to keep it cool, the building cost £12,000 and could once accommodate up to 1,500 people. Refurbishment followed a fire in 1887 and improvements included plush upholstery, velvet hangings and a magnificently painted ceiling. From 1884 to 1926 it operated as a touring venue for opera companies including the D'Oyly Carte, and was indeed called the Opera House.

The mini-skirted actress left stage of the Royal Theatre marks this as a 1960s scene. Roger Lloyd Pack, next to her, earned fame as Trigger in *Only Fools and Horses*. The photograph is by Brian Douglas, who in the 1950s was a friend of the theatre manager John Ellins. He asked him to stand in for the stage carpenter for a fortnight, the carpenter never came back and Brian stayed 32 years, doing photography as well.

The Northants Candy Queen contest at the Salon de Danse, 1965. Teenager Suzanne Rollestone, fourth from the left, doesn't look too pleased at coming second out of six contestants, all of whom had to be connected with the confectionery trade. The winner worked in a sweet shop, while Suzanne's father kept the Marefield sub-post office and newsagents.

There are few more relaxing sights than a village cricket team at play. Here is Cogenhoe's team, down from the hills and posing in immaculate whites on the racecourse in 1968. The team includes Brian Foley, Les Robjohns, Geoff Waldren, Bob Sketchley, George Adkins, Brian Godsiff, Ted Mann, David Bliss and Alf Merritt. Horse racing ceased on the course generations earlier, following serious accidents; the Jockey Club pronounced it unfit for racing in September 1904 – but happily for turf enthusiasts, Towcester is only eight miles away.

Jim Drinkwater walking down the track from Heyford Loop to visit his mother. Above him are the overhead cables that were soon to 'bring Northampton closer to London'. He saw some tough times on the railways, but remembers brighter moments, too: 'We'd fry eggs on the shovel. It was cleaned in the red hot fire-box, better than a plate!'

Driver Jim Drinkwater and fireman C. Lewis on the footplate of a Class 8F loco on Heyford Loop, early 1960s. Jim recalls: 'Tearing along in the steam, it was a job to see the signals, not like on the electrics, where you run over a magnet and hear a buzzer. It was more dangerous. Returning from Bicester once, we hit a tractor and trailer crossing the line and smashed it to smithereens, killing the farmer.'

King Edward VII Hospital, now Northampton General, May 1964. There was no National Health Service until 1948, and before that time the poor often suffered. The philanthropic shoe magnate James Mansfield set up a hospital at Western Favell, which was later amalgamated with the General. Western Favell specialised in the treatment of crippled children, and this photograph was loaned by Gordon White, who was the last shoe-maker to be employed there.

Council houses at Far Cotton. Old Cotton used to have very much a village atmosphere and all seems quiet enough here, with few cars, grass verges and picket fences.

Clun Castle at the head of a special excursion train through Castle station in March 1965. The driver was Fred Bateman from Bletchley, who had served 31 years with LMS before nationalisation. The Castle class had been one of the most durable of express locos, originated by the Great Western in the inter-war years and built right through to 1950 by the nationalised British Railways. By 1965, however, its remaining engines were on the verge of extinction in the public sector, and this excursion was organised by Ian Allan, publishers of the train spotters' 'bibles'.

Suzanne Rollestone in a fashionably short skirt in summer 1966 at the family's holiday retreat near the present Billing Aquadrome. There were about 40 chalets on the site, along with caravan spaces, and Suzanne has happy memories of its wonderful views.

Sainsbury's site in Abington Street being developed in June 1962, as Northampton felt the first major tremors of the 1960s upheaval. Even in 1925, however, the Mawson Report, published by planning consultants engaged by the town council, concluded: 'Northampton's opportunity lies in having good foundations on which to build the new Northampton of the future.' The aim of the report was to make proposals for regulating future growth in the interests of industrial efficiency, convenience and amenity.

Labour's Minister of Housing and Local Government, Dick Crossman, engaged consultants on a similar task. On 3 February 1965 he announced to the House of Commons that, together with Ipswich and Peterborough, Northampton had been selected for a major expansion scheme to accommodate a planned intake of 70,000 people from London by 1981, followed by natural growth after that. The pattern followed the 1952 New Towns Act and ideally, new legislation was needed to lay down the ground rules for a working partnership between the government and a local body of the size and status of an all-purpose county borough.

The urgency of the situation did not permit this, however, and instead, Crossman appointed Messrs Wilson and Womersley as agents to recommend an area near or in Northampton for major expansion. In this way, the special powers of the New Towns Act could be used to transform the old town centre, as well as to find extra space near by. After a process of proposals, consultations and objections, implementation of the scheme was placed in the hands of a separate Development Corporation.

Market Square, June 1962. Welsh House, the main building in this picture, dated from 1595 and was one of the few properties to survive the Great Fire of 1675; people trapped by flames in the Square escaped through its doors into the orchard behind. The *Northampton Herald* had offices here during the nineteenth century, while in 1962, before demolition, Tuckey's was one of several businesses sharing the premises. Just above its window is a feature incorporating John Parker's family arms, inscribed in Welsh: 'Without God, without anything; with God, enough.' A pastiche of the building's original gabled frontage has been incorporated in the Grosvenor Centre redevelopment.

The *Chronicle and Echo*, commenting on the changes befalling Northampton, wrote in January 1968 : 'From now on it will mean big thinking and imaginative planning so that in the words of the inquiry report, the community spirit shall not be lost.' This picture shows Gold Street in May 1963, before the improvements. The area suffered great damage in July 1941 when a Stirling bomber crashed here.

The Royal Theatre production of *No No Nanette* in 1969, with Helen Worth front right. She is now far better known as *Coronation Street*'s Gail Platt.

Meanwhile, the daily theatre of life continues on the cobbled market square in 1969.

The Sensational
Seventies

Northampton power station's redundant cooling towers are blasted into dust as 1970s changes accelerate. Local man Baden Powell worked for the Northampton Electric Light Company from 1936 and has mixed memories, remembering the general foreman as 'a proper old tyrant'; the company had started in 1891. Janet Wooding remembers swimming in neighbouring Midsummer Meadow open air pool in the 1950s: 'It was filthy, with smuts from the power station and basic changing cubicles, but we liked it.' Inevitably, the pool went.

The New Town Commission planned new estates on Briar Hill, power substations, pylons, underground TV cables and other paraphernalia of modern life, but these were stringent times, and a proposal from the London Quadrant housing trust for low-cost homes there was rejected by the NTC in 1977. Better drainage was a priority, and in April 1976 the Development Corporation agreed to give £1.78 million to the River Nene Washland Scheme, which could not be further delayed. Cheaper than the original Nene Barrage Scheme, it allowed an area of the river valley to flood during peak rainfall, with water released under control through sluice gates and locks.

Other priorities included two large speculative office developments, increasing town floor space to 900,000 square ft by March 1976; new factory and warehousing space totalled 3,825,000 square ft. The first section of the Nene Valley Way high-speed road opened in 1976, increasing the length of new roads laid locally since 1970 to 22 miles. West Hunsbury was preparing for 2,500 homes for 12,000 people and East Hunsbury more than 2,500 homes for 8,000. Large numbers of young people would obviously be moving in, and preparations were made for expected increases in anti-social behaviour by some of them. In January 1977 the Development Corporation was concerned that rent arrears were 26 per cent, compared with the borough's 13 per cent, and said it felt this reflected changing attitudes and socio-economic conditions.

The 1970s were days of hippy rebellion, IRA terrorism, racial strife and finally the coming to power of the controversial Margaret Thatcher. The decade was also a time to learn that our small-town preconceptions about strangers were in need of a radical overhaul. Brian Douglas, who worked at the Royal Theatre, recalls: 'Two people with very strange haircuts and bangles all over the place visited regularly. My wife Audrey had shown them to their seats. She said: "You should talk to them, they're very well spoken, polite and knowledgeable about the plays."'

Wanda Moore as Lady Touchwood from the Royal Theatre's June 1970 production of *Double Dealer*. This is another study by Brian Douglas, who became a Fellow of the Royal Society for Theatrical Portraiture in 1969. Brian said: 'Weekly rep was hard on the actors. When we did *Oliver*, I resurrected a revolving stage from Coventry. Because I made it work, Coventry wanted it back – but our show was so successful that we were able to buy our own, ready for the Christmas production in 1968.'

Below left: Tom Osborne Robinson was head of design at the Royal Theatre for 49 years. He is remembered as a great theatrical painter who loved doing things on a grand scale.

Below right: Rex Robinson in the Royal Theatre's March 1971 production of Dryden's *All for Love*.

A Wesley bus crew at Mayorhold, May 1971. Wesley's grew apace during the Second World War, even though it was difficult to get parts. Bob Wesley even worked to repair a bus on his wedding night – and fell down the inspection pit.

Carnival Parade, June 1971, with an Allchin 10-ton steamroller, built in 1900 and restored by Bert Henman of the borough engineer's department. William Allchin, general engineers and brassfounders, originated in Merton, Surrey, in 1847 and were renowned for steam lorries and rollers. Local firms such as Hamp's and the Gold Street furniture store Jeffery's, as well as the Corporation, were among their customers.

Northampton House dominates the skyline in this town centre view of July 1972. In the foreground and on a more human scale are flats for those fortunate enough not to be on the lengthening housing queues.

As Northampton House looms large on the right side of the picture, a new pattern of roads is imposed on the central area. The old is not quite obliterated, however, and there are one or two tenuous reminders of the town our forefathers knew.

The Parade was the name given to this row of buildings on the north side of the Market Square, previously known as Cornhill, in its dying days of summer 1972. This is the site of the old Emporium Arcade, which housed Church's glass and china outlet. A campaign to save the buildings collected 10,000 signatures and support from the National Victorian Society, but to no avail. Church's was relocated in the new Welsh House, while Abel's old-established music shop ceased trading. The corner of the old *Chronicle and Echo* building is just visible on the right. The *Northampton Mercury* was printed here from 1730 to 1978, and it was this building that Bradlaugh's supporters attacked in the riots of 1874. It was redeveloped for C&A, with the newspaper moving to the Mounts.

Church's glass and china shop and the entrance to the Emporium Arcade shortly before demolition. Not all businesses could afford the new rents around here after redevelopment.

The Cattle Market entrance in September 1975, during its long, steady decline. Gordon Pell remembers it as a boy before the war: 'I used to take cattle to market on Saturday for Mr Griffith, and had to get up at five to drive them down Towcester Road, along St Leonard's Road, over the railway level crossing and into market. He paid me sixpence, which I passed to my mum.'

Looking south from Delapre Abbey, 1970. Built in 1145 and dissolved by Henry VIII in 1538, the abbey and grounds eventually passed to the Bouverie family. When the last of these died in 1943, the property was bought by the council. The building was taken over by the record office in 1958 and the grounds became a public park.

Iron and steel used to flourish in the north of the county, but industry suffered rapid decline through EEC quotas, recession and the McGregor cuts. Here a redundant quarry engine is hoisted on to a C. Butt low loader for delivery to the Peterborough Railway Preservation Trust in the 1970s.

A Wednesday lunchtime in February 1974, and a Roe-bodied Corporation Daimler bus turns from Lady's Lane into Sheep Street. This is JVV 213, one of a group of five bought in 1958 and close to the end of its active life, though it looks smart enough in the new standard livery introduced in 1973.

Demolition of railway arches near St John Street station on the Wellingborough line, January 1973. A whole world of bonded warehouses and Victorian terraces, customs and curiosities went under the sweeping hammer blows of the dragline – the tracked vehicle in the centre of the picture.

It might look like something out of the old TV sitcom *On the Buses*, but to some this was no laughing matter: the last bus and crew from Derngate bus station, 1 May 1976, the 11.05 p.m. Duston Circular. The vehicle is a Bristol VRT, registration number SRP 817N and one of a group of six. Derngate was an exclusive stop for National Bus vehicles, usually the local United Counties.

Central Northampton, looking north across the gas works, December 1973. The old racecourse is visible at the top of the picture, but the landscape has become increasingly dominated by high-rise buildings and main roads dividing it into sections.

The central clearance area, July 1972, with the Church of the Holy Sepulchre prominent in the background. Hard lives were lived on these streets, but perhaps those who look for ways in which the people who lived in them could be said to be part of 'the good old days' conclude that while they were struggling for a basic existence, they at least had less time to be bored, disruptive or jealous. The key question is: would you happily have changed places with them?

The town viewed from the Carlsberg Brewery site, May 1977, with the gentle waters of the canalised river rippling past. The tanneries were near here long ago, and the British Chrome Tanning Company was based in Grafton Street. Chrome tanning suited the production of leather for mass-produced shoes.

A long-wheelbase AEC Marshall tipper from C. Butt's fleet loading gravel at Earls Barton pit during the late 1970s. In the early days, hauling tanned leather from London and Liverpool was the company's main business, the hides having been imported mainly from India.

July 1972, and Northampton House rises hideously or majestically, depending on your viewpoint, close to the old Fancier's Working Men's Club in Wood Street. The twelve-storey building was completed at a cost of £12 million.

Greyfriars bus station from the tenth floor of Northampton House, September 1978. A Corporation Alexander-bodied VRT bus emerges in front of a Daimler/Roe, while a United Counties VRT is far right. The foreground is the site formerly occupied by the Fancier's Working Men's Club.

An aerial view of central Northampton in June 1974, with the Guildhall making a fine centrepiece. The town had changed greatly since the *Chronicle and Echo* had written in January 1968: 'Expansion of Northampton has been given the go-ahead under the New Towns Act with only slight cutting back in the land takeover made in the draft designation order . . . designating some 19,952 acres of land in and around the town as part of the plan to provide homes for 70,000 Londoners by 1981, increasing Northampton's population to 220,000.'

There were protests. Gordon Pell, who gave up his apprenticeship with the City Press to join the Royal Navy, settled in Duston after the war, and enjoyed the village atmosphere. He says: 'We put a banner across the street saying: "Hands off Duston", but they took no notice. Village life wasn't the same afterwards.' Farmland beyond was protected, however, and the newspaper reported: 'The Minister was obviously impressed by the strength of opposition to the prospective loss of good agricultural land and this "concession" will doubtless give great satisfaction.' The editorial ended: 'If all goes well it should prove an exciting journey, particularly for the younger generation who will grow up to a new inheritance so different from the old.'

The Hurtful Eighties and Naughty Nineties

The Drapery in 1980, and the consumer society is in high gear for Christmas. Margaret Thatcher is Prime Minister, and an inspiration to a new breed of career women. Her messages were anti-trade union and pro-deregulation and hard work. Industry was to become leaner and fitter, national unemployment was to rise and Northampton Development Corporation aimed to ensure that it did not do so locally by providing an extensive programme of industrial development. In June 1981 it reported that factory space totalled 1,800,000 square ft, 850,000 of which was partly obsolete.

Mrs Thatcher insisted that unions and red tape frustrated development and aimed to ease planning restrictions. Profits would rise, and those in work would be better off. The downside was that soon there were signs of an underclass, homelessness, more racial strife and declining standards in public services. Northampton's distinctive red corporation buses and green United Counties would vanish with the 1985 deregulation of buses, all in the name of profit and efficiency.

Industrial action was harshly dealt with, and fortunes were made as the economy shifted to services and old local shops gave way to more multiples. St James retail park was the shape of '80s shopping, and a far cry from the cotton mill there a century earlier.

The Christmas Prime Stock Show at the Cattle Market, December 1980. There was no BSE to worry about, and this beast's services were doubtless much sought after.

Disasters always draw crowds. Here they are breaking up after a fire at the Wedgwood Restaurant, then part of the Berni Inn chain, in Abington Street, July 1984. Policeman David Brown and bus driver Bryan Spence saved two men trapped in the blaze, climbing on to the roof of a double decker to pull manager Nino Bartella and chef Derek Smart clear. Rubbish piled outside the building the night before appeared to have been the cause.

Fire-fighters tackle a blaze on the sixth floor of Beaumont Court in April 1984, by which time they were well versed in the problems posed by high-rise flats. Their job can involve times of tedium interspersed by life-threatening danger, but former fireman Dave Wilson, who joined the brigade after a disastrous winter as a roofer during the big freeze of early 1963, says: 'There were highs and lows – but I never had that Monday morning feeling.' Northampton's first volunteer brigade was formed in 1864.

Mid-1980s, and nurse Jean Powell, a teetotaller, is bemused by an apparent gift of alcohol on retirement from Northampton General Hospital. There were fewer smiles all round in July 1999, when the hospital was said to be struggling with debts of £2.6 million.

John Walker at Turner's Musical Merry-Go-Round in 1984. 'People were sceptical when Nigel Turner opened at Wootton,' he says. 'It looked like a big barn from outside, but it was a great success. I enjoyed working there.'

Coach entrepreneur Bob Wesley at his home in Sywell in March 1998 – the instrument that graces his sitting room these days being a world away from the accordion he played as a boy.

Bob and Gwen Wesley with memorabilia from Wesley Bros, who sold out to York's when Bob was seventy. His father started the business, and he was known to take cigarettes among other things in lieu of payment. Bob's enthusiasm for machines extended to luxury cars such as Bentleys and Aston Martins and he has even flown a Tiger Moth from Sywell Aerodrome. Now in his nineties, he attributes his success and long life to hard work.

Demolition in 1991 of Barry Road shoe factory, originally known as the Panthers, then Sears Tru-Form and Burlington's. A scheme to build flats on the site was rejected and the Co-op bought it for a car park. Shoe-maker Gordon White recalls its reputation as one of the better factories in which to work.

The scaffolding collapsed during demolition at Barry Road, but complete disaster was averted by a sturdy lamp-post and prompt action by a worker who shinned up poles and tightened a few bolts. Rummaging in the rubble afterwards, Gordon White found a sad memento – a copy of the *Burlington Bugle*, issue 5, dated February 1989, which said: 'Last month we told you about showrooms we were creating at 51 Maddox Street to launch our shoes at home and overseas. In addition we intend to use the street level and basement as a small, prestigious shop to illustrate the quality merchandise available from our factories.'

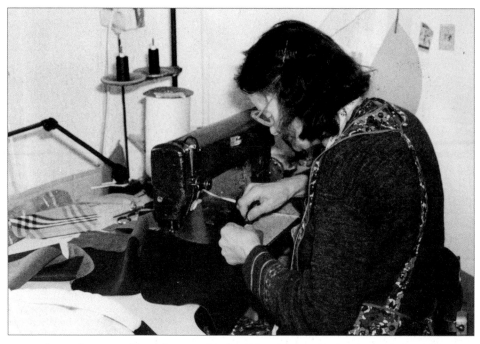

Nose to the grindstone at Fink's Northampton factory. Sylvia White is pictured sewing leather coats, the work was hard on the hands and as if that were not bad enough, workers were not allowed to listen to the radio.

Sylvia White (left) at her retirement party at Fink's factory, 1990. She spent all her working life there making leather coats, including some extremely opulent designs for wealthy clients.

Abington Street on a cold February morning, 1996. The message on the shop window is: 'Everything Reduced.' Hard though life was in past times, the sight of people sleeping on the streets was virtually unknown to previous generations.

This lady feeding pigeons in Abington Street in winter 1995 was doing her bit for wildlife struggling in an urban world. However, she was photographed not long after shoppers were warned by the council's environment committee chairman that feeding is cruel, encouraging pigeons to breed up to six times a year and adding to town centre health hazards.

Gasometer in Towcester Road, and in front of it, hoardings spinning dreams to whisk you away from such a harsh urban environment – a sleek French car or a win on the National Lottery.

Doris Ward with her late sister Connie's copy of the history of the Royal Theatre and Opera House, signed by famous showbiz names including the Hollywood film star Gregory Peck.

Two happy faces waiting at the mini-cab office in Bradshaw Street. Race relations in Northampton tend to be reasonable, though without the slightest cause for complacency.

Busker, Abington Street, spring 1999: 'I like to see the children dance the hokey-cokey while I play.'

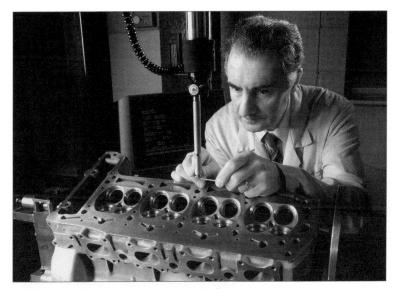

A good racing driver needs the best equipment. These are the experienced hands of Cosworth Engineering's Ted Dawson measuring a Mercedes cylinder head at the company's St James Mill Road workshops in around 1990.

Twice World Formula One Champion, Michael Schumacher with racing and design teams at Cosworth's factory, February 1994. They are posing behind the Cosworth Ford Formula One-Zetech-R V8 engine, which powered his Benetton B194 to his first World Championship.

Best of rivals: Damon Hill and Michael Schumacher at the post-British Grand Prix press conference at Silverstone, just a few miles from town, 1994. Damon won, although both men look equally disgruntled.

Former World Formula One Champion turned team boss Jackie Stewart (right) at the opening of Cosworth's HQ at Costin House, September 1988. He is with company founder Keith Duckworth OBE (left) and co-founder and chairman from 1988 to '90 Mike Costin.

The great red dream machine: Michael Schumacher and his Ferrari – every schoolboy's idea of what a racing car should look like, whatever its success rate – prepare for British Grand Prix practice at Silverstone in 1994.

Home win: proud Damon Hill celebrates his triumph in the British Grand Prix, 1994.

There's the odd Brazilian flag, the odd Ferrari banner – but the union flag and slogans in praise of Damon Hill dominate this crowd scene after the 1994 British Grand Prix.

It won't stay this way: Schumacher's B194 Benetton leads the 1994 British Grand Prix, tailed by the Austrian Gerhard Berger's Ferarri and Hill's Williams – number zero.

Rubbish waiting to be cleared after the 1994 British Grand Prix; 55 cleaners spend a week clearing spectator terraces after the big race. More than 22,000 three-course meals are served at Silverstone over the four days, 128 helicopters shuttle VIPs and team crew on and off the circuit – and in 1999 there was a surprise extra flight to take an injured Michael Schumacher to Northampton General Hospital.

111

Market Square, looking at the Christmas lights from outside Welsh House, December 1998. There's still a traditional festive look about the market stalls.

Con and Dec of the Irish singing group the Bachelors autograph photographs for a new generation of fans at a 1960s charity nostalgia concert in Derngate in December 1998. Derngate opened in 1983 and is one of the best and most versatile multi-purpose venues in Britain. It has been the scene of major international shows such as *Aspects of Love*, *Buddy*, *Phantom of the Opera* and Glynebourne Touring Opera productions. The auditorium is remarkably flexible with a proscenium stage for theatre, a flat floor for exhibitions, an arena style made famous by televised snooker tournaments and as a concert hall acclaimed by classical and rock musicians alike.

Pronuptia Bridal and Men's Formal Wear Shop in York Road, early 1999. Pretty mannequins in flouncy dresses evoke a fairytale, but the average British marriage lasts just nine years and ten months. Mind you, most people do it all over again soon after the divorce. . . .

Northamptonshire's own fairytale princess, the former Diana Spencer of Althorp, attending a function not far from her family home, February 1983. She still has the air of innocence apparent during those early days of marriage to Prince Charles, before the dream faded. Because of her long lineage in the county, it is said that her two children are the most 'English' royals for more than five centuries.

A sex shop in Abington Square, offering aids to bring romance and excitement back into relationships. Another point of view is that such goods are degrading; there is certainly an almost inevitable outcry from potential neighbours when planning permission is sought for these outlets.

A bleak scene in Abington Street, February 1996. A scarcely noticed newsboard announces: 'Charles and Diana, Bishop Speaks.' The subject is their proposed divorce, but passers-by do not seem to want to know. How different from Northampton's Charter Year of 1989, when Diana was a popular visitor as she became the town's first royal Honorary Freeman.

South Bridge, election day, 1 May 1997, and the country is about to agree that Enough is Enough as far as John Major's Conservatives are concerned. John Prescott arrived on the Labour battle bus and declared that things had got to change. Doubtless not everything that has changed since then has pleased all the electorate, but at least Mr Prescott was up there addressing the crowd; by and large, old-style rallies with politicians facing the mob and up for scrutiny have long gone.

General election rallies used to take place in the Market Square, and Labour could rely on fair support from the working man in the 1950s. The Labour traditionalist R.T. Paget won by a walkover in the 'Never had it so good' Tory success of 1959; he was still there in 1974 when all the changes were under way, and Labour were enthusiastic about the big movements of overspill to Northampton and Milton Keynes.

A canal leisure boat chugs along near the brewery in July 1997. Floods have been a problem in the area, causing tragedy, and in July 1999 the Environment Agency announced packages totalling £17 million to relieve the problem. Floods at Easter 1998 killed two people and damaged thousands of homes.

Above: Shooting gallery at John Scarrott's fair at Kingsthorpe, February 1999. John's father started in fairs in the 1950s, though his Welsh great-grandfather was running boxing booths locally a couple of generations before that. In between times, Henry Thurston was famous for Northampton fairs. *Left*: Mrs Scarrott in the pay booth of the dodgems. 'Fairs are as popular as ever,' say the couple. 'All right, *you* might have grown out of them – but there's always a new generation coming along.'

Salvation Army bandsmen, Market Square, spring 1997.

Balloon Festival, race course, August 1998. The balloons float graceful and free, but there's a hard-edged commercial message on them.

Students, too, are not the bright-eyed idealists they once were; after all, there are no cushy grants these days. The girl, from Newcastle University, is selling rag mags, and there's nothing very new about that. What *is* different is the fact that she is with not a college friend but a marketing man from the publishers.

117

William Butt in 1992, still a guiding hand in the family haulage firm he co-founded, and which has prospered since into contract vehicle leasing. He says: 'When we were nationalised I became manager, but I bought two of my old vehicles from the new organisation and ran them under a different name within the allowed distance limits. That way I continued servicing local customers. You needed a special permit to go beyond a 25-mile radius from base, and the railway companies always objected if you applied for one. Road haulage won in the end because it reduces handling times.'

Looking back on changes in his home town of Northampton he says: 'As a lad I can remember Saturday mornings seeing cattle driven through the main road of St James, to and from market. Drovers were a regular sight, with cattle coming mostly from Ireland via Liverpool to Far Cotton station. Those that weren't sold were driven to Hillmorton in Rugby on foot. They were a smashing sight, about fifty of them taking it easy. Those drovers were a rare old breed. Today everybody is in such a hurry to get everywhere. There's no doubt people used to be more friendly. You knew each other more, though life was hard.'

Anna Murby, afternoon show presenter, in the BBC Radio Northampton studio. Her job also involves getting out and about interviewing local people.

Councillor Alwyn Hargreaves is among those enjoying all the fun of the merry-go-round at St Crispin's Fair in 1994.

Young people of the town relaxing around the shoe-makers sculpture in Abington Street in June 1999. Their future will doubtless lie in a working environment far removed from the shoe factories that were once synonymous with Northampton.

Nursing Sister Ann Gloag and her brother Brian Souter created the Stagecoach bus empire out of a sideline. Deregulation in 1985 created their opportunity to buy United Counties and bring in some of their old London buses, which are pictured standing redundant at Rotherthorpe Road depot in 1997.

Mereway Upper School, with two mobile phone company masts on site – a novel way of raising funds to cope with shortages. Doubts have been raised, however, about the advisability of siting them so near to a school.

Traffic jam on the A508, which had been planned as a high-speed road on the east of town. It is estimated that road delays cost Britain £19 billion a year – and the solution to the problem is one of any number of improvements to our life that we could hope for in the new millennium.

Acknowledgements and Picture Credits

Many people have helped or influenced and contributed to this book, and there is not room to thank them all adequately. My wife Nicola did much of the editing. Inevitably, I have read many books on Northampton, and with no wish to imitate them, I could not fail to be impressed by much that has been written, particularly by Alan Burman, who has covered the town in so much detail. My particular interest is the 1960s and '70s developments, and I must acknowledge the influence on my understanding of Jeremy Seabrook's work *The Everlasting Feast*.

I am very grateful to all who contributed their time and knowledge to this project, but stress that they are not responsible for any of its shortcomings. It is not always apparent from the text how much an individual has helped; Brian Hensman from the museum encouraged my earlier study and introduced me to Gordon White; Suzanne and Terry Tarpley pointed me along some interesting avenues of inquiry and went out of their way to help; Andrew Shouler's expert advice, guidance and additional research have also been invaluable.

Every reasonable effort has been made to contact photograph copyright holders, and acknowledgement is made to all of them. Without the kindness of people who loaned pictures there would be no book. I am also very grateful to the *Northampton Chronicle and Echo* for permission to use past issues for research and quotes.

Contributors: Dominic Allard, B. Barton, G. Blane, M. Blane, Pip Brimson, the late Dr W. E. Brocklehurst, *Buckingham and Winslow Advertiser*, C. Butt, G. Butt, P. M. Chisholm, Church & Co. plc, F. Coles, S. Collier, N. G. Cook, N. J. Cook, Cosworth Archives, Derngate Theatre, B. Douglas, J. and M. Drinkwater, C. Dunn, Express Lift Co., D. George, K. Gibbins, M. Gibson, B. Hensman, C. A. Hodgkinson, I. M. Kennedy, J. Martell, L. Miller, New Towns Commission, Northampton Borough Council, Northamptonshire Business Link, Northamptonshire County Record Office, Northamptonshire Fire and Rescue, Northants Royal Navy and Royal Marines Association, Northampton Machinery Company, Jake McNulty, J. Ounsworth, R. Patrick, B. Peet, G. Pell, A. Pillans, Baden Powell, P. Reynolds, Royal Theatre and Opera House, Sinead Ryan, Mr and Mrs J. Scarrott, J. Seabrook, A. Shouler, L. R. Smart, W. H. Smith, C. Stacey, Stoke Goldington Archive, S. and T. Tarpley, J. Walker, Doug Ward, Doris Ward, R. Watson, R. and G. Wesley, Gordon White, S. White, Y. White, D. E. Wilson and J. Wooding.

PHOTOGRAPHS

Photographs were kindly loaned by the following, though the fact does not necessarily imply that they are the copyright holders. Page numbers are given, with the key: t: top; c: centre; b: bottom; l: left; r: right.

Martin Blane: 58tl. Pip Brimson: 102b, 103b. *Buckingham & Winslow Advertiser*: 70b, 109b, 110tr, 111 all, 117bl, 119t. C. Butt Ltd: 54b, 59 all, 95t, 98b, 118. Church and Co. plc: 6, 25b, 62b. Fred Coles: 44, 45 both, 53. Simon Collier: 23tl & tr, 48t, 63, 66 both. R. Cook: front and back endpapers, 19, 20 all, 24b, 26bl & br, 27bl & br, 28bl & br, 31t, 32b, 34b, 35t, 36–7, 104c & b, 107 all, 108t & b, 112t & b, 113t & b, 114t & b, 115, 116 all, 117t & br, 119b, 120 all. Cosworth Engineering: 109t & c, 110tl. Brian Douglas: 50tl, bl & br, 51b, 52t, 82b, 88t, 90 all. Jim Drinkwater: 41t & b; 54t, 64t, 80t, 84tl & tr. Colin Dunn: 64b, 68t & b, 79. Express Lift Co.: 25t, 32t, 34t, 57, 58tr & b, 60t, 61t & c, 65t, 67t & b, 69t, c & b, 89. Northampton Borough Council: 2, 56t, 61b, 73, 74, 75b, 77b, 78br, 80c, 81t, 82t, 84b, 85t, 86, 87t & b, 88b, 91b, 92t & b, 93t & b, 94t & b, 96t, 97t & b, 98t, 99t, 100, 101, 102. Northampton County Record Office 49t, 51t. *Northampton Chronicle & Echo*: 78t, 96b. Judy Ounsworth: half title page, 13, 21, 22t & bl, 24t, 27t, 28t. Robin Patrick: 85c. Baden Powell: 39t. Pam Reynolds: 42b, 43, 62t, 71. Andrew Shouler: 80b, 91t, 95t, 99b. R. Staniford: 38b. S. Tarpley: 75t, 76, 77t, 78bl, 81bl, 83t, 85b. T. Tarpley: 65b, 83b. Gordon White: title page, 23b, 26t, 29t & b, 30t & b, 31bl & br, 33, 35b, 38t, 39b, 40t & b, 46t, 49b, 50tr, 55t, 56b, 105t & b, 106t, 107b, 119c. Gordon White & Peter Rideout: 48b. John Walker: 104t. Doris Ward: 46bl. Doug Ward: 46br, 52b. Doug Ward & Roland Holloway: 47. Doug Ward & Colwyn Photos: 72t. Bob Wesley: 42t, 55b, 70t, 72b. Dave Wilson: 103t.